Teaching Grades K–12
with the Internet

A companion Web site for this book is maintained at:
URL: http://twi.classroom.com/grades/k12/

Teaching Grades K–12 with the Internet

Internet Lesson Plans and Classroom Activities

By Timothy P. Dougherty & David N. Kershaw

classroom
CONNECT

2221 Rosecrans Ave., Suite 221
El Segundo, CA 90245
URL: http://www.classroom.com
Email: connect@classroom.com
(8 0 0) 6 3 8 - 1 6 3 9

Senior Editor/Project Lead: Kathleen Housley
Editor: Marianne Clay
Design: John Svatek
Production Designer: Jay Walters
Manufacturing: Benjamin Cintas

Corporate Office
2221 Rosecrans Ave., Suite 221
El Segundo, CA 90245

Product Development Office
1241 East Hillsdale Blvd., Suite 100
Foster City, CA 94404

All terms mentioned in this book that are known to be trademarks
or service marks have been appropriately capitalized.

Printed in the United States of America

3 4 5 6 7 8 9 10   02 01 00 99 98

ISBN 0-932577-45-8

Product Code: TWI-1000

Contents

Preface   ix
About the Authors   x

Language Arts 1

Grade Level   Lesson Plan   Page

9–12   Hamlet on Trial: Innocent, Guilty, or Insane? . . 2

K–4   Ladle Rat Rotten Hut: Jabberwocky for Kids. . . . 6

7–12   Masculine/Feminine Word Choices. 10

5–8   Poetry in Motion 14

7–10   The Poet's View of Death. 18

8–10   Romeo and Juliet: A Production
        Company Simulation. 22

6–12   Sensory Images in Poetry. 28

9–12   William Shakespeare: Bard or Bogus?. 32

Grade Level   Activity Sheet   Page

9–12   Aging and the Poetry of W.B. Yeats 36

7–10   His and Hers: Two Views of Love 38

K–4   Wormy Poetry 41

Mathematics 43

Grade Level   Lesson Plan   Page

8–12   Exploring π. 44

7–9   Geometric Probability 47

2–6   It's the Method that Counts 51

4–6   Let's Paint! 54

9–12   Similar Triangles. 57

8–12   Solving Word Problems. 61

Science 65

Grade Level   Lesson Plan   Page

9–12   Acceleration and the Earth's Gravity 66

4–8   The Great Sharks: Misunderstood and on Trial! 71

6–9   Lab Lightning 74

3–6   Microscope: Find the Pictures 78

8–12   Tour the Circulatory System 82

4–6   We Love Cockroaches! 85

K–4   Worms: Nature's Recyclers 89

Grade Level   Activity Sheets   Page

4–8   Meteor Puzzle 93

4–12   Surviving a Lunar Crash 97

2–4   A Tale about Cockroaches 100

K–6   Walk the Dinosaur through Time 102

Social Studies   103

Grade Level   *Lesson Plan*   *Page*

| 6–10 | Archaeological Time Capsule. . . . . | 104 |

| 9–12 | Balancing the Budget . . . . | 108 |

| K–4 | Learning Japanese . . . . | 111 |

| 4–8 | Seven Wonders: Past and Present . . . . | 114 |

| 5–9 | Symbolism in Architecture . . . . | 118 |

| 9–12 | *Titanic:* Unsinkable?. . . . . | 122 |

| 4–8 | Virtual Family Tree . . . . | 125 |

| 10–12 | War Letters . . . . | 128 |

Grade Level   *Activity Sheets*   *Page*

| 5–8 | Pictures from the Past. . . . . | 131 |

| 8–11 | Athens Travel Brochure . . . . | 135 |

Glossary   137

Lesson Plans, Organized by Grade Level   141

Preface

As you've probably discovered, it's one thing to navigate the Net and find great education material, and it's quite another to integrate the Internet into your classroom curriculum in a timely way.

This book helps you get your classroom jumpstarted on the Information Superhighway. We've done the legwork for you. We supply hands-on, step-by-step methods for incorporating the Internet into your curriculum. We've put together a sampling of the best lesson plans from *Classroom Connect's* newsletter and our Educator's Internet CD Club to get you and your students on your cyberspace journey today.

Teaching Grades K–12 with the Internet features four sections: Language Arts, Mathematics, Science, and Social Studies. The lessons have been arranged in alphabetical order. The suggested grade levels are simply guidelines, and most can be modified for use in other grades. Many of the lesson plans feature extensions for additional student activities. There are reproducible student handouts and stand-alone activity sheets for students to use independently or in small groups.

As an added feature, we maintain a Web site with hot links to all the sites featured in this book. That way if any URL address changes, you will have the latest Web address so you and your students wouldn't be delayed or detoured. The Web site address is:

URL: http://twi.classroom.com/grades/k12

Kathleen M. Housley
Senior Editor, *Classroom Connect*
Email to: khousley@classroom.com

About the Authors

The *Classroom Connect* staff writes and produces books, newsletters, CDs, videos, and other teacher-created materials for educators worldwide. The Classroom Connect members who developed and edited the curriculum for this book are Timothy P. Dougherty David N. Kershaw, and Marianne Clay.

 Timothy P. Dougherty taught both language arts and music theory in grades 7–12 prior to joining the *Classroom Connect* staff as a curriculum developer. He now writes educational content for the *Classroom Connect* newsletter, the *Educator's Internet CD Club,* and other publications and projects.

 David N. Kershaw—a secondary school math teacher with a special interest in physics—develops math and science curriculum for the *Educator's Internet CD Club* and other publications. A graduate of Millersville University, he taught mathematics and science in grades 7–12 before joining the *Classroom Connect* team.

 Marianne Clay has written stories for *The New York Times* and *The Baltimore Sun,* served as managing editor for *The Hudson Review,* and taught high school English. A graduate of Hood College, she is now editor of the *Educator's Internet CD Club,* a CD-ROM product that offers Internet sites and curriculum for K–12 teachers.

Language Arts

Lesson Plans,

Activity Sheets,

and Student Handouts

A Note on the Organization

Lesson plans are arranged in alphabetical order, with grade levels indicated in the top left corner.

Student handouts are included with some of the lesson plans and are identified with a computer icon on the top left-hand corner.

Stand-alone activity sheets appear at the end of the chapter.

LESSON PLAN	# Hamlet on Trial
Grades 9–12	Innocent, Guilty, or Insane?

Overview

Your students will gain a deeper, more enriching understanding of *Hamlet* after putting Hamlet, the protagonist, on trial for the multiple murders in the play. This lesson is best introduced at the start of your *Hamlet* unit and implemented when your students complete their study of the play.

Materials

- Props for court room drama (optional)

Objectives

- Use details, clues, and examples from the text to formulate a case for or against Hamlet
- Analyze and assume the roles of court figures
- Engage in the trial of Hamlet
- Deliberate a verdict and possible sentence based on the "facts" from the text

Procedures

1 Most of us have a difficult time understanding the complexities of a trial until we're part of the process whether as defendant, plaintiff, or jury member. We might read about a crime and a conviction, but we rarely follow the steps in a trial. This lesson offers the opportunity to experience how a trial works.

Your students have probably watched *The People's Court* or *Court TV* on cable. Some of them might have followed the sensationalistic media coverage of the O. J. Simpson trial. Ask your students to share their feelings on the U.S. judicial system. Ask your students, through a show of hands, how many think that our justice system is effective or not, fair or not. Try to uncover as many angles and "not-thought-of" items in this process.

2 Tell your students to read the play, *Hamlet*, very carefully and to list character traits of Hamlet as they read. The entire play can take weeks of class time to read and discuss, so remind them daily to take the initiative to collect pertinent data. Perhaps a graded nightly journal entry would help your students stay on task.

Hamlet
URL: http://the-tech.mit.edu/Shakespeare/Tragedy/hamlet/
      hamlet.html

3 Introduce the figures involved in a trial and the roles they serve, from the judge to the bailiff. Be sure all students get an active role. There are more than enough roles to fill! Make sure that your students understand their courtroom roles for this trial. Set a date for the trial well into the future so your students have enough time to research both their roles and the play. Remember, as in a court of law, only the facts are admissible. Determine if Hamlet is innocent, guilty, or insane, or any combination of these. Two trials never yield the same results. Remember, Shakespeare left no answers.

4 On the specified date, hold the trial. If possible, videotape the trail. Videotaping the student trial will be an invaluable resource for your future classes, as well as being a great way for your current students to review their work.

Extensions

1 You can research the facts and hold trials for other Shakespearean tragic heroes. Consider, for example, Othello, Romeo, Macbeth, Julius Caesar, or Brutus. You can find all these plays, with helpful annotations, on the Internet.

Julius Caesar

URL: http://the-tech.mit.edu/Shakespeare/Tragedy/juliuscaesar/juliuscaesar.html

Romeo and Juliet

URL: http://the-tech.mit.edu/Shakespeare/Tragedy/romeoandjuliet/romeoandjuliet.html

Othello

URL: http://the-tech.mit.edu/Shakespeare/Tragedy/othello/othello.html

Macbeth

URL: http://the-tech.mit.edu/Shakespeare/Tragedy/macbeth/macbeth.html

❷ Compare and contrast the O. J. Simpson trial to *Othello*. Your students can get a fresh perspective on the play and on the Simpson trial by linking these two figures together. Discuss the themes and situations with your students and have them compose an essay exploring the similarities and differences.

Othello

URL: http://the-tech.mit.edu/Shakespeare/Tragedy/othello/othello.html

❸ While your class is in a deliberative mode, why not put William Shakespeare on trial? There has been a long standing debate on who actually wrote the plays: a Stratfordian named William Shakespeare or an Oxfordian earl. Send your students to the library to research both sides of the argument and make their own decision. The more familiar your students become with the works, life, and times of William Shakespeare and of Elizabethan England, the more they'll be able to support their conclusions.

The Shakespeare Mystery

URL: http://www.pbs.org/wgbh/pages/frontline/shakespeare/

Shakespeare Oxford Society

URL: http://www.shakespeare-oxford.com

Hamlet on Trial

Innocent, Guilty, or Insane?

- Read *Hamlet* very carefully and,as you read, list the character traits of *Hamlet*. Since this play is long and complex, spend a little time on it every day. You might want to keep a journal for collecting your notes each day.

Hamlet
URL: http://the-tech.mit.edu/Shakespeare/Tragedy/hamlet/hamlet.html

Ladle Rat Rotten Hut

Jabberwocky for Kids

Overview

In this lesson, your students will experience how meanings can be assembled from nonsense words.

Materials

- Multimedia computer with speakers or sound capability
- Tape recorder

Objectives

- Decipher the story based on reading and listening to it several times
- Convert a story into "jabberwocky"
- Create "jabberwocky" words and sentences

Procedures

1 Your young students probably invent new words in their everyday conversations with their friends. How do they "know" what a word means if they've never heard it before? What happens when your students encounter a new word, as they most likely do every few minutes, from a book? Can your students piece together a denotation from the words that surround the new word? Could your students determine a word's meaning from hearing a speaker use intonation and inflections with their vocal delivery? This lesson will prove that they can! Ask your students to contribute some of their "original" words and describe the object or circumstance that their word defines. Keep track of the words, phrases, and expressions on the blackboard.

2 Go to the *Ladle Rat Rotten Hut* site on the Internet and have your students read through the story text on screen. Chances are, your students may feel a bit confused after one silent read, so read the story aloud to them next.

Ladle Rat Rotten Hut
URL: http://www.exploratorium.edu/imagery/exhibits/ladle/
    ladle.html

Ask your students if hearing you read the story cleared some of the confusion. Did hearing the words help your students to get a clearer picture of the story? Some of your students may recognize that the story is actually *Little Red Riding Hood*, but with jumbled nonsense words. Ask your students how they generated words from the plot of this story, especially if they are all "jabberwocky" words. Let them explain how they came to such conclusions.

3 Listen to the online oral interpretation of *Ladle Rat Rotten Hut* at the *Ladle Rat Rotten Hut* site on the Internet. Then repeat step two.

Ladle Rat Rotten Hut (Real Audio)
URL: http://www.exploratorium.edu/rafiles/ladle.ram

This story is read with intonation and vocal inflections that reflect the meaning and placement of the words. A question is inflected upward; an emphatic statement is read with stronger conviction.

4 Have the class rewrite the story into the contemporary English that your students use to speak to each other.

⊞ Extensions

1 Have your students bring in a copy of their favorite fairy tale (Ask them to chose a short one.) Then have them exchange the copies of the story with their classmates. The students can rewrite the stories with nonsense words as illustrated in *Ladle Rat Rotten Hut*. Have your students exchange their rewritten stories to yet another student to decipher. Compare the original story with the final interpretation of the story by the third student. This exercise occurs in real life every time someone has to translate a document into another language. You may even want to record your students reading each other's "translated" stories for a fun activity. Use the recorded examples to highlight the idea of vocal delivery. Your student would love it and learn as well!

❷ For another famous example of nonsense words in action, obtain a copy of Lewis Carroll's "Jabberwocky" or one of Dr. Seuss's books. Repeat the steps of this lesson with those examples.

❸ Have your students record a conversation they have with their friends. Then ask them to listen to the words and select which ones their parents, teachers, older siblings, etc., may not understand. Ask your students to define these words and teach them to the class. Of course, you'll have to ensure that the words are not "objectionable."

❹ For a real stretch, go to the Real Audio speeches by the Clinton administration on the Internet and convert them to "gibberish" language, while retaining the feel and delivery of the speech. Sometimes one can piece together what a speech in another language is about by listening to the delivery and emotion of the speaker. Read and listen to the speeches.

Vice President Al Gore
URL: http://www.whitehouse.gov/WH/EOP/OVP/html/
GORE_Home.html

Some of the President's Recent Public Addresses
URL: http://www.whitehouse.gov/WH/EOP/OP/html/
OP_Speeches.html

Ladle Rat Rotten Hut

Jabberwocky for Kids

- Go to the *Ladle Rat Rotten Hut* site and read through the story text on screen.

Ladle Rat Rotten Hut
URL: http://www.exploratorium.edu/imagery/exhibits/ladle/ladle.html

- Listen to the online oral interpretation of *Ladle Rat Rotten Hut* at the *Ladle Rat Rotten Hut* site.

Ladle Rat Rotten Hut (Real Audio)
URL: http://www.exploratorium.edu/rafiles/ladle.ram

Masculine/Feminine Word Choices

Overview

This lesson focuses on identifying gender-specific language in poetry and determining whether such language offers a valid way to express ideas.

Materials

- Dictionaries and thesaurus
- Blackboard or overhead for generating a class list

Objectives

- Analyze gender-biased writing
- Interpret *Filling Station* by Elizabeth Bishop
- Rationalize student choices of gender-laden words

Procedures

1 Ask your students if any writing can be truly free of gender-bias. Cite such examples as vessels named after women, the word "mankind," the word "history," etc. Are these specific references to male/female the only gender-specific examples in our language? Many of the Romance languages, from which English derives, have gender specified by the case ending of the words. Ask your students to compile a list of nouns, verbs, adjectives, and adverbs, which distinctly ring masculine or feminine to them. Ask your students to tell why. For some background and more gender-related writing situations, go to the *Purdue Online Writing Lab's Non-Sexist Language* page.

Non-Sexist Language
URL: http://owl.trc.purdue.edu/Files/26.html

Keep a list of your students' reactions and word choices in this exercise.

❷ With this warm-up in gender-specific language fresh in your students' heads, have them read *Filling Station* by Elizabeth Bishop on the *American Literature Survey* site. Have them read the poem silently and have them read the poem aloud in small groups. Urge them to always read and listen to the words of any poem!

Filling Station
URL: http://www.cwrl.utexas.edu/~daniel/amlit/poetry/
        fillingstation/fillingstation.html

❸ Discuss the elements of poetry to aid your students in understanding this poem, but focus on the word choice of the poet for this lesson. Here, Bishop makes many references to "femininity" without being obvious. Bishop also defines "masculinity" without being condemnatory. Have your students list the masculine-sounding words and the feminine-sounding words from the poem.

Ask your students to decide whether or not the poem paints a fair picture of the differences between man and woman. Let your students use their imagination and assure that no one's feelings will be hurt in this exercise. Perhaps the young men and women in your class will gain a better understanding of the point of view of the opposite sex. When your students have completed their lists and rationalizations, have them share with the class. Then ask a volunteer to read the poem aloud once again and discuss it as a class. Ask your students to determine who is the "somebody" that takes care of the flowers and "...loves us all." Is it a gender issue or not? You may use this prompt to take your discussion to the level of the poem as allegory.

⬛ Extensions

❶ Look for specific words in some of the other poems on the *American Literature Survey* site in the Poetry section at the Internet site for the same gender-specific language, whether it is implicit or explicit, and carry out a similar lesson.

American Poetry

URL: http://www.cwrl.utexas.edu/~daniel/amlit/poetry/
    poetryenrollment.html

❷ Choose some local or national newspaper articles. Ask your students to look for some of the words they've chosen from the Elizabeth Bishop poem, and see if the usage in the newspaper articles carry the same connotation as they did in the poem.

❸ Read *Young Goodman Brown* by Nathaniel Hawthorne. Look for the relationship and gender-specific language used to describe the character's names, actions, and relationship between Brown and his wife, Faith. This will take much more time to complete than the poem because this is a short story, so you might need to set aside several periods for this activity. Have your students deliberate in groups, and make each group responsible for several paragraphs.

Young Goodman Brown

URL: http://www.cwrl.utexas.edu/~daniel/amlit/goodman/
    goodman.html

Masculine/Feminine Word Choices

- For some background on gender-related writing situations and on gender-biased words, go to the *Purdue Online Writing Lab's Non-Sexist Language* page on the Internet.

Non-Sexist Language
URL: http://owl.trc.purdue.edu/Files/26.html

- Read Elizabeth Bishop's poem. Notice the words she selects to describe femininity and masculinity.

Filling Station
URL: http://www.cwrl.utexas.edu/~daniel/amlit/poetry/fillingstation/fillingstation.html

Poetry in Motion

 Overview

This lesson takes the text of a poem and brings it to life through motion, drama, and the improvisational use of props.

 Materials

- Ordinary and extraordinary items of little value
- Bags
- Video camera (optional) or other media equipment as per student need and availability

 Objectives

- Interpret a poem
- Dramatically interpret a poem
- Make a presentation with props and other ordinary items
- Explore symbolism and connotation

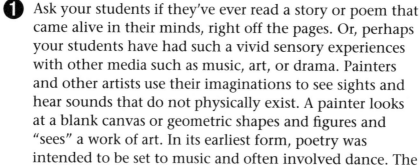 **Procedures**

1 Ask your students if they've ever read a story or poem that came alive in their minds, right off the pages. Or, perhaps your students have had such a vivid sensory experiences with other media such as music, art, or drama. Painters and other artists use their imaginations to see sights and hear sounds that do not physically exist. A painter looks at a blank canvas or geometric shapes and figures and "sees" a work of art. In its earliest form, poetry was intended to be set to music and often involved dance. The arts were merged. But since these early days, the arts have become separate entities.

Give your students a short Rorshach Test with some words from the dictionary. Choose a few words, both common and esoteric, and ask your students to share their first impression or mind's eye vision of what these words connote. You'll notice that these words often mean different things to different people. Your students may provide you with unique sensory definitions for the same word.

2 Group your students into fours and have them briefly surf through these sites to find a short (1 page maximum) poem that they would like to present as a group. You can help them find appropriate poems.

English Poetry
URL: http://www.staff.uiuc.edu/~d-gao/english.html

Shakespeare: Sonnets
URL: http://the-tech.mit.edu/Shakespeare/works.html

Robert Burns
URL: http://www.ece.ucdavis.edu/~darsie/burns.htm

The Poetry of Yeats
URL: http://www.maths.tcd.ie/pub/yeats/Index.html

Dylan Thomas
URL: http://pcug.org.au/~wwhatman/dylan_thomas.html

3 After each group has selected a poem for their group, have them read the poem to each other and discuss its meaning. Walk around the groups and offer suggestions and thought-starters, but permit your students to go where they will with this lesson. Explain that each group will dramatize the poem the next day in class. One student in each group will read the poem, while the others act it out. Also tell each student to bring ten objects, chosen at random, for use as props in the dramatic poetry presentations. Before the dramatic presentations, the students will exchange their things, so no one knows which objects their group will be using as props. This activity provides a creative exercise in visualizing, dramatizing, improvising, and exploring a poem. Plan to allow your student groups one class period to get their props and prepare their short dramatizations.

4 Present and videotape the presentations and allow your student groups to have a few moments to explain why they dramatized the poem in the way they did. This discussion will convey your student groups' understanding to the class and to you. Have students critique each other's presentations and their own. Ask them to consider what they might do differently had they more time.

⚇ Extensions

❶ For more dramatic exercises, try to devise some improvisations for your students. You may wish to select a famous scene from a play, such as the balcony scene from *Romeo and Juliet* or one of Prince Hamlet's soliloquies from *Hamlet*. Have your students rewrite the scene into modern language with modern props.

Romeo and Juliet
URL: http://the-tech.mit.edu/Shakespeare/Tragedy/romeoandjuliet/
romeoandjuliet.html

Hamlet
URL: http://the-tech.mit.edu/Shakespeare/Tragedy/
hamlet/hamlet.html

❷ Have your students repeat the steps of this lesson, but instead of dramatizing the piece, have your students select or, better yet, compose an accompanying piece of music to be played while the poem is read. Or, your students can select music from any genre for this activity, not just the classics. Why not team-teach with your music department for this activity?

❸ Have your students read the poem *Fern Hill* by Dylan Thomas and find pictures capturing the essence of the poem's setting. Or have them create their own "mental picture." Many poets write masterful verse, after gaining insight and inspiration from beloved surroundings. Wordsworth had Tintern Abbey. I have Indian River Inlet. Your students have their favorite place as well! Ask your students, having read the poem, to consider their place and write a poem about it. Ask them to develop sounds and art to accompany their poems. Your students can turn in their "multimedia" reports and share/compare them with their classmates.

Fern Hill
URL: http://www.mcp.com/people/mulder/fernhill.html

Poetry in Motion

- To find a poem to use for your group presentation, look at these sites:

  English Poetry
  URL: http://www.staff.uiuc.edu/~d-gao/english.html

  Shakespeare: Sonnets
  URL: http://the-tech.mit.edu/Shakespeare/works.html

  Robert Burns
  URL: http://www.ece.ucdavis.edu/~darsie/burns.htm

  The Poetry of Yeats
  URL: http://www.maths.tcd.ie/pub/yeats/Index.html

  Dylan Thomas
  URL: http://pcug.org.au/~wwhatman/dylan_thomas.html

- After your group selects their poem, read and discuss the poem's meaning. Then your group should prepare to dramatize the poem for a class presentation.

The Poet's View of Death

Overview

This lesson compares and contrasts how a variety of poets treat the theme of death in their works.

Materials

- Blackboard or overhead projector
- Knowledge of basic poetic elements

Objectives

- Analyze various poetic genres and styles
- Cite differences/similarities among the selected poems
- Explore tone and theme as literary devices
- Work effectively in small groups

Procedures

1 Poetry is not exclusively for writers and "wits." It is written by humans, for humans, and deals with "nothing new under the sun." Tell your students that even the greatest poets merely wrote about topics and themes that everyone who breathes has the propensity to understand: love, fear, hope, loss, envy. Write a list of emotions and feelings on the blackboard, and ask your students for a show of hands on whether they have felt these. Chances are these topics are nothing new to your students, yet many language arts students claim no ownership in poetry, saying that it is "too hard to understand." If you begin your studies of poetry with a common theme, the rhetoric and devices of poetry can be seen to augment the poem's central theme, rather than detract from its accessibility.

❷ Group your students into pairs or threes, and have them select one of the poems from the list below. Have them read through the poems and look for words, feelings, images, instincts, and gut feelings that connote or denote death. Some of these poems take a hopeful tone toward the passing of life, and some are bitter. All humans have mixed emotions regarding death. Your students will as well. Ask your student groups to take notes on their findings and subsequent discussions with their peers.

Sir Patrick Spens
URL: http://www.staff.uiuc.edu/~d-gao/ballad1.html

Dirge
URL: http://www.staff.uiuc.edu/~d-gao/shakesp3.html

When I Consider How My Light Is Spent
URL: http://www.staff.uiuc.edu/~d-gao/milton1.html

Elegy Written in a Country Churchyard
URL: http://www.staff.uiuc.edu/~d-gao/gray1.html

The Little Black Boy
URL: http://www.staff.uiuc.edu/~d-gao/blake.html

Ulysses
URL: http://www.staff.uiuc.edu/~d-gao/tennison3.html

The Soldier
URL: http://www.staff.uiuc.edu/~d-gao/brooke1.html

Do Not Gently Into That Good Night
URL: http://www.staff.uiuc.edu/~d-gao/thomas1.html

September Song
URL: http://www.staff.uiuc.edu/~d-gao/hill1.html

Epitaph
URL: http://www.staff.uiuc.edu/~d-gao/yeats1.html

❸ After your students read their poems and take notes, have the groups disassemble. Ask each student to silently read the text and determine the author's tone and message regarding death. Ask each student to write a paragraph about what the poet is saying about death in that poem. The students can base their paragraphs on the results of their collected data, their group readings and discussion, and their silent reading.

4 Ask each student to read their paragraph aloud. In this way, the students will determine how much they agree and disagree about the intended tone and meaning of the poetry. See how much the members of the each group agree or disagree.

Extensions

1 Ask your students to consider their favorite novel, film, or comic book, and to describe in one word its theme. Make sure your students explain their choices for theme. For example, "hope" could be a one-word example of a theme. These themes exist in all works, from literature to music to art! The more adept your students become at deciphering themes, the deeper their appreciation of the work.

2 Have your students compose a spontaneous poem on the theme of loss or separation. They could write about a first-hand experience, such as a lost possession, friend, or pet. If they prefer, they could imagine the scenario. It could even be humorous. Let your students convey the tone they wish and urge them to maintain this tone through-out their poems, unless, of course, their feelings change while they are composing!

3 Repeat the steps of this lesson, but center on the topic and themes of love. There are several great starting points from which your students can explore the many faces of love through poetry. Start with some of these classic poems of love.

Astrophel and Stella
URL: http://www.staff.uiuc.edu/~d-gao/sidney1.html

Leave Me, O Love
URL: http://www.staff.uiuc.edu/~d-gao/sidney2.html

Amoretti Sonnet One
URL: http://www.staff.uiuc.edu/~d-gao/spenser2.html

Sonnet 18

URL: http://www.staff.uiuc.edu/~d-gao/shakesp2.html

Sonnet 116

URL: http://www.staff.uiuc.edu/~d-gao/shakesp1.html

Song to Celia

URL: http://www.staff.uiuc.edu/~d-gao/jonson1.html

❹ Every culture marks death, but the ancient Egyptians focused on death. Send your students to this Egyptian site and the school or local library for more information.

The Institute of Egyptian Art and Archaeology

URL: http: //www.memphis.edu/egypt/main.html

The Poet's View of Death

- After you and your group select your poem, discuss the poem. How does this poem treat death? List the words of the poem that express death and that express the tone of the poem.

Sir Patrick Spens

URL: http://www.staff.uiuc.edu/~d-gao/ballad1.html

Dirge

URL: http://www.staff.uiuc.edu/~d-gao/shakesp3.html

When I Consider How My Light is Spent

URL: http://www.staff.uiuc.edu/~d-gao/milton1.html

Elegy Written in a Country Churchyard

URL: http://www.staff.uiuc.edu/~d-gao/gray1.html

The Little Black Boy

URL: http://www.staff.uiuc.edu/~d-gao/blake.html

Ulysses

URL: http://www.staff.uiuc.edu/~d-gao/tennison3.html

The Soldier

URL: http://www.staff.uiuc.edu/~d-gao/brooke1.html

Do Not Gently Into That Good Night

URL: http://www.staff.uiuc.edu/~d-gao/thomas1.html

September Song

URL: http://www.staff.uiuc.edu/~d-gao/hill1.html

Epitaph

URL: http://www.staff.uiuc.edu/~d-gao/yeats1.html

<table>
<tr><td>LESSON PLAN</td></tr>
<tr><td>Grades 8–10</td></tr>
</table>

Romeo and Juliet
A Production Company Simulation

 Overview

This lesson challenges your students' ability to visualize and imagine. Your students will read a text and make sensory assumptions as they create the balcony scene in *Romeo and Juliet*.

 Materials

• Vivid imagination

Objectives

• Compare elements of drama and film production
• Interpret a scene from a William Shakespeare play
• Collaborate with a small group in a reader's theater rendition of the play excerpt
• Imagine and create a set, actor list, and other production proposals for the scene

Procedures

1 Ask your students to imagine themselves as playwrights or screenplay writers who have just finished writing their masterpieces. What happens next? If your students wish to have their work published and performed, what are the necessary steps? Your students must consider the set, the costumes, the actors and actresses, the soundtrack, and special effects as well as the budget and the time allowed to complete the project. Major motion picture and production companies usually contract some of the many tasks to specialized professionals in the field, but they have the luxury of a big budget. Your students are operating under a tight budget, and they have to devise a way to produce their work cheaply, but effectively. This activity will open your students' minds to the complex process of production.

❷ Have your students assemble in small groups under the premise that each is competing for the contract to produce one scene from a Shakespeare play to get their big break into the world of production. Each group must perform a reader's theater version of the scene to get acclimated with the variables and possibilities of the text. Then each group should submit their proposals for set, location, actors, music, etc., as well as their rationale for each choice. Your students must become intimate with the text and allow their imagination, coupled with the grounding effects of a limited budget, to create the best possible production in a very short time. Your students will not be performing the play, but they will be paying close attention to detail as they consider the production elements.

Have your student groups go to the famous balcony scene from *Romeo and Juliet* for this assignment.

Romeo and Juliet Act 2, Scene 2
URL: http://the-tech.mit.edu/Shakespeare/Tragedy/romeoandjuliet/
    romeoandjuliet.2.2.html

You and your student groups can evaluate and critique the production suggestions to determine which production group to "hire" to produce the full play. Remind your students that both time and money are in short supply. After all, the production company needed to be chosen yesterday!

❸ Ask your student groups to read through the balcony scene and to explore the possibilities of production. Make sure they include all the elements that would be necessary for performance, whether it be filmed or performed live in a theater. Your students are free to take artistic license with this scene, if they so desire. For example, this scene may be set into a different, modern location, with a modernized approach to the script. Let their imaginations run wild!

4 Let your student groups deliver their proposals orally the next class period, so they will have enough time to read through the scene and complete their production proposals.

5 Take a vote on the most effective, ingenious production of the scene, but praise each group's efforts! "The play's the thing..."

Extensions

1 Follow the steps of this lesson, but this time, use these brief lines from Macbeth. Your students can hear a dramatic interpretation of these lines at these Web sites as well.

Macbeth Audio File
URL: http://aitg.soc.uiuc.edu/poetry/macbeth.AIFF

Six Lines From Macbeth
URL: http://www.staff.uiuc.edu/~d-gao/macbeth.html

2 Allow your students to choose a scene from another famous Shakespeare play from this site on the Internet which contains the complete works of Shakespeare. Your students could rewrite one of the scenes into the informal language they speak with their friends. Shakespeare is frequently performed with a modern English script, and these plays provide a highly entertaining as well as fresh approach to the Bard's plays.

The Complete Works of William Shakespeare
URL: http://the-tech.mit.edu/Shakespeare/works.html

3 Have your students check the artistic and dramatic renditions of Shakespeare plays at these sites.

William Shakespeare, Harper Audio
URL: http://town.hall.org/Archives/radio/IMS/HarperAudio/
020994_harp_ITH.html

Shakespeare Illustrated
URL: http://www.cc.emory.edu/ENGLISH/classes/
Shakespeare_Illustrated/Shakespeare.html

4 Guide your students through the steps of this lesson, but this time your students will become the Elizabethan production company working for William Shakespeare himself. The play must be produced in the Globe Theater. Your students can take a virtual tour of the Globe to acclimate themselves to this famous theater.

The Rebuilding of Shakespeare's Globe Theater
URL: http://www.delphi.co.uk/delphi/stories/9508/16.Globe/
intro.html

Romeo and Juliet
Production Company Simulation

- Read the balcony scene from *Romeo and Juliet* and decide, with your group, how you can best produce this scene.

- Consider set, location, actresses and actors, music, costumes, props, etc.

- To arrange the production details, you and your group must become intimate with the text. Pay close attention to detail and your budget as you consider the production elements. Then use your imagination to create the best possible production proposal. Have fun!

Romeo and Juliet Act 2, Scene 2
URL: http://the-tech.mit.edu/Shakespeare/Tragedy/romeoandjuliet/romeoandjuliet.2.2.html

Sensory Images in Poetry

Overview

This lesson explores the role and effectiveness of sensory descriptions and images in poetry.

Materials

- Computer with Internet access
- Vivid imagination!
- Sensory awareness

Objectives

- Read and orally interpret *The Red Wheelbarrow*, a poem by William Carlos Williams
- List the sensory images in the poem
- Fill in other "missing" sensory details and descriptions
- Compose an original sensory poem

Procedures

1 Ask your students to freewrite for 3 - 5 minutes about a place that is special to them: perhaps the place where they feel the most safe and secure. You can freewrite as well. Students love to hear their teacher's innermost thoughts as well! When your time is up, ask for volunteers to describe the place to the class. Note how often your students use sensory details such as sight, sound, touch, taste, and smell. The more sensory details included, the more vivid the "picture" a writer can paint. How much needs to be left to the imagination?

❷ Go to *The Red Wheelbarrow* by William Carlos Williams, at the American Literature Survey Site

The Red Wheelbarrow
URL: http://www.cwrl.utexas.edu/~daniel/amlit/poetry/
    wheelbarrow/wheelbarrow.html

Ask your students to read through this brief poem once. Then ask a volunteer to interpret the poem aloud. Discuss the poem using some of the thought starters on *The Purdue Online Writing Lab's Thought Starter* site. While these prompts work with any writing activity, this poem lends itself to wide, reflective, personal interpretation.

Thought Starters
URL: http://owl.trc.purdue.edu/Files/101.html

The suggestions on this site will help your students think more deeply about the words in this poem and to explore the sensory applications of a simple red wheelbarrow and white chickens. Deliberate about why "so much depends upon" these simple things. Could these words evoke memories, smells, feelings, etc.? Could these words be merely "art for the sake of art?"

❸ As a class, fill in some of the "missing" sensory details from the poem. Since the poem uses minimal visual details, try to determine what the scene smells, tastes, feels, or sounds like. Your students can also include the memories or internal feelings they associate with the scene in *The Red Wheelbarrow*. Allow your students to be personal, imaginative, and reflective.

❹ Have your students expand *The Red Wheelbarrow* by adding words expressing their senses and feelings to the original text. Ask them to compose in and around the original text, weaving in dependent clauses, descriptive adjectival, adverbial phrases, and colorful prepositional phrases. For additional writing help in these areas, go to the *Purdue Online Writing Lab's* Web site called:

OWL Handouts in Outline Form
URL: http://owl.trc.purdue.edu/by-topic.html

Have your students share their new, personal poems based on *The Red Wheelbarrow* with the class. Then tell them to put their poems in their student writing folders.

✿ Extensions

❶ Ask your students to compose an original sensory poem, perhaps based on the scene in their freewrite. Make sure your students include all sensory details of sight, sound, touch, and smell as well as any other memories or personal thoughts. Ask your students to consider how they would describe this scene accurately to someone who is blind, deaf, etc.

❷ For more practice in sensory writing from another angle, go to the *Civil War* site's Civil War Photos from the Library of Congress and have your students write a poem or descriptive essay about what they think the scenes in the photos sound, feel, taste, smell, look like in color, etc. Ask your students to also consider how the subjects of the photos are feeling. What thoughts are going through their minds?

The Civil War Collection
URL: http://rs6.loc.gov/ammem/cwarquery.html

Sensory Images in Poetry

- Read *The Red Wheelbarrow* by William Carlos Williams, on the *American Literature Survey* site

The Red Wheelbarrow
URL: http://www.cwrl.utexas.edu/~daniel/amlit/poetry/wheelbarrow/wheelbarrow.html

- This poem lends itself to personal and reflective interpretation. For more ideas about ways to think about poetry, go to the *Purdue Online Writing Lab's Thought Starter* site.

Thought Starters
URL: http://owl.trc.purdue.edu/Files/101.html

William Shakespeare

Bard or Bogus?

Overview

Students use higher level critical thinking skills to form a thesis on the mystery of Shakespeare as author of his works.

Objectives

- Determine the author of a short poem
- Read several Shakespeare texts and gather background information on Shakespeare and his time
- Research and collect data on the mystery of Shakespeare as author of his works
- Employ critical thinking skills
- Take a side: Stratfordian or Oxfordian, based on the strength and weakness of each side's argument based on the texts and historical issues
- Compose an essay illustrating the main points of each side's argument

Materials

- Computer with Internet access, a WWW browser, and Newsgroup software
- Shakespeare texts: several plays

 # Procedures

❶ Read a famous, but fairly obscure poem to your class and claim authorship over the poem. Ask your students to critique the poem, thinking that you are the author. Keep track of their responses. Reveal the true author of the poem; now ask your students to critique the poem. See if their responses change. Ask your students how easily or how often this could happen in the world of the literary canon. There are always mysteries that shroud the issue of authorship in the printed word over time: the case of William Shakespeare is possibly the most ongoing and heated! Make sure that your students have some experience with Shakespeare's works before completing this lesson.

❷ Have your students go to these sites on the World Wide Web to gather information on the debate that still rages. Have your students amass a list of the main points of each side's argument, as well as the refutations against these points. Ask your students to keep notes on the "players" involved in the mystery as well.

The Shakespeare Mystery
URL: http://www.pbs.org/wgbh/pages/frontline/shakespeare/
    index.html

The Shakespeare Mystery: Update
URL: http://www2.pbs.org/wgbh/pages/frontline/shakespeare/
    tindex.html

The Oxenford Reader
URL: http://www.shakespeare-oxford.com/oxenford.htm

Shakespeare Oxford Society Home Page
URL: http://www.shakespeare-oxford.com/

Shakespeare Authorship News
URL: http://www.shakespeare-oxford.com/evernew3.htm

Why Stratfordians Are so Stubborn
URL: http://www.shakespeare-oxford.com/shak2.htm

Computer Tackles Shakespeare Mystery
URL: http://www.sciencedaily.com/old/2-17-96/shake.htm

3 When your students have had ample time for research, discuss the main points of the mystery and the arguments presented as a class. This session will ensure that all your students have found enough data to build their own case and share their findings with each other.

4 Assign an essay to each of your students: a substantive, opinionated essay that illustrates your students' view of the who actually wrote the works of Shakespeare. Ask your students to assume the roles of members of a jury, working with "just the facts" and how well they are presented, then they must make a decision based on these propositions.

5 Post your student essays to this Usenet Newsgroup and let some contemporary Shakespearean experts comment on your students' work, and to join in a raging debate! Educators and professionals frequent this newsgroup, so there will be feedback!

Contemporary Shakespearean Usenet Newsgroup
URL: news:humanities.lit.authors.shakespeare

Extensions

1 Your students could arrange a mock trial with William Shakespeare as the defendant. Have your students use the material from this lesson and the background legal information on this site to round out your trial. Videotape the trial and have your students critique it.

Legal Dictionary
URL: http://www.wwlia.org/diction.htm

2 For further study, be sure to supplement your knowledge with these "starting points" to rich Shakespearean sites on the Internet.

Mr. William Shakespeare and the Internet
URL: http://www.daphne.palomar.edu/shakespeare/

Surfing with the Bard
URL: http://www.ivgh.com/amy/

3 Have your students investigate plagiarism, passing of someone else's work as your own, by visiting these sites on the Internet. What are some of the ramifications of plagiarism? Could someone be plagiarizing in the Shakespeare mystery?

Ursinus College Statement on Plagiarism
URL: http://lib.ursinus.edu/~libweb/plagiarism.html

Plagiarism
URL: http://www.austlii.edu.au/arkady/unsw/faculty/
    procedures/sec11.html

Attitudes Toward Plagiarism
URL: http://arts.uwaterloo.ca/ENGL/courses/engl210e/
    210e/wkt/sec_204.htm

Aging and the Poetry of W. B. Yeats

Student name:_____

Step	A

Every person is unique, with unique ideas about the experiences shared by all people: birth and death, love and rejection, success and failure. Read through these three poems by William Butler Yeats, a celebrated Irish poet, and answer the questions about the themes an aging Yeats presented in these three poems.

The Folly of Being Comforted
URL: http://www.maths.tcd.ie/pub/yeats/TheFolly.html

1. What is Yeats's view of aging in this poem, and what does he mean by the "folly" of being comforted?

_____

_____

_____

_____

The Old Men Admiring Themselves in the Water
URL: http://www.maths.tcd.ie/pub/yeats/TheOldMen.html

2. How does the view of aging change in this poem? Is this a hopeful or regretful poem in your opinion? Support your answers.

_____

_____

_____

36

Activity Sheet   Aging and the Poetry of W. B. Yeats
···

A Prayer for Old Age

URL: http://www.maths.tcd.ie/pub/yeats/PrayerForOldAg.html

3. Are the themes of the previous two poems applicable to this poem as well? What do you think that Yeats is saying about his fear of aging?

_____

_____

_____

_____

Step	B

Now that you've explored the themes of aging you've found in these three poems, select the poem most similar to your thoughts about aging. Compose your own poem with your ideas about aging using the poem you have selected as a model.

Step	C

Share your poem with the class and discuss!

His and Hers

Two Views of Love

Student name:_____

Step | **A** Not only the poets realize that women and men seem to view love differently, and that these different outlooks can cause some discord in relationships! Read through the two sonnets below, and try to determine the gender of the poet based on the clues and assumptions you draw from the text.

Sonnet 32
The first time that the sun rose on thine oath
To love me, I looked forward to the moon
To slacken all those bonds which seemed too soon
And quickly tied to make a lasting troth.
Quick-loving hearts, I thought, may quickly loathe;
And, looking on myself, I seemed not one
For such man's love! — more like an out-of-tune
Worn viol, a good singer would be wroth
To spoil his song with, and which, snatched in haste,
Is laid down at the first ill-sounding note.
I did not wrong myself so, but I placed
A wrong on thee. For perfect strains may float
'Neath master-hands, from instruments defaced —
And great souls, at one stroke, may do and dote.

Sonnets from the Portuguese

URL: http://www.inform.umd.edu:8080/EdRes/Topic/WomensStudies/ReadingRoom/Poetry/
    BarrettBrowning/SonnetsFromThePortuguese/the-first-time-that

Sonnet 18
Shall I compare thee to a summer's day?
Thou are more lovely and more temperate:
Rough winds do shake the darling buds of May,
And summer's lease hath all too short a date:
Sometime too hot the eye of heaven shines
And often is his gold complexion dimmed;
And every fair from fair sometimes declines,
By chance or nature's changing course untrimmed;
But thy eternal summer shall not fade,
Nor lose possession of that fair thou ow'st;
Nor shall death brag thou wander'st in his shade,
When in eternal lines to time thou grow'st:

So long as men can breathe, or eyes can see,
So long lives this, and this gives life to thee.

LudWeb
URL: http://www.ludweb.com/msff/sonnets/mssonnet18.html

Step	B

Answer the following questions

1. Which sonnet was written by a woman? Support your answer with specific examples from the poem.

_____

_____

_____

_____

2. Now look at the poem you believe was written by a man. What particular words and phrases, in your opinion, tell you the author's gender?

_____

_____

_____

_____

Step	C

Ask your teacher to reveal the gender identities of the two poets. Were you correct? if you were incorrect in your assumptions, what words and phrases "threw you off?" Now put gender differences aside, and write briefly about the themes of love you found common to both poems.

_____

_____

_____

Activity Sheet   His and Hers: Two Views of Love

Step | D

Write a sonnet praising yourself, but write from the point of view of the opposite sex. If you are male, write the kind of sonnet an admiring female would write. If you are female, write the kind of sonnet a male student might write to compliment you. Remember Shakespeare, Browning, and a host of other poets often chose to bring honor to someone they liked by writing a sonnet. Enjoy this opportunity to honor yourself!

Step | E

Check out these Sonnet sites for further information and inspiration.

An Index of Poem Titles in Representative Poetry: S – U
URL: http://utl1.library.utoronto.ca/disk1/www/documents/utel/rp/indextitles_stu.html

The Sonnet
URL: http://www.english.upenn.edu/~afilreis/88/sonnet.html

The Sonnets
URL: http://the-tech.mit.edu/Shakespeare/Poetry/sonnets.html

Wormy Poetry

Student name:_____

Step	A

Go to the *Worm World-Poet's Corner* site. Read and listen to the poems written about those squiggly, creepy-crawly little things that we find in the street after it rains — worms!

Worm World-Poet's Corner
URL: http://www.nj.com/yucky/worm/gallery/poetry.html

1. Why would someone want to write a poem about a worm? How do you feel when someone hands you a worm?

_____

_____

_____

Step	B

Write your own poem about a worm now that you've read some other writers' poems about worms. Use these words at the end of each line to help you rhyme! Make the first letter of the first word of each line capitalized.

_____ worm

_____ dirt

_____ germ

_____ shirt

_____ ground

_____ slimy

_____ grimy

_____ around.

Activity Sheet Wormy Poetry

Step	C

Share your poem by reading it, slowly and clearly, to the class.

Step	D

Perhaps your teacher can record you reading your poem with a tape recorder that can be played back at different speeds. If you speed up the tape, the pitch of your voice will rise, and you'll sound a little like a squirmy worm!

Mathematics

Lesson Plans,

Activity Sheets,

and Student Handouts

A Note on the Organization

Lesson plans are arranged in alphabetical order, with grade levels indicated in the top left corner.

Student handouts are included with some of the lesson plans and are identified with a computer icon on the top left-hand corner.

Stand-alone activity sheets appear at the end of the chapter.

Exploring π

Overview

In this lesson, students discover the value of π and its relationship to the parts of a circle by using induction and estimation.

Materials

- Paper

Objectives

- Discover properties of, and relationships between, figures from given assumptions
- Represent and solve problems using geometric models
- Estimate answers to problems from derived data

Procedures

❶ Go to *Graphics for the Calculus Classroom*. Tell your students to travel to *Archimedes' calculation of* π and view the movie on the page.

Graphics for the Calculus Classroom
URL: http://www.math.psu.edu/dna/graphics.html

Archimedes' calculation of π
URL: http://www.math.psu.edu/dna/graphics.html#archimedes

2 Have your students inscribe polygons inside circles. They should increase the number of sides with each inscription. Assuming that the radius of each circle is one, your students can find the area of each polygon.

3 Your students will begin to realize the area of each polygon is getting closer to the area of each circle. Have your students put their findings on charts. Since the radius of each circle is assumed to be one, they will discover the areas are approaching the value of π.

Extensions

1 Your students can follow the same methods with circumscribed polygons with the numbers gradually decreasing to π. For more advanced classes, do circumscribed and inscribed polygons at the same time. This will give them an upper and lower boundary from which to estimate π.

2 Another exercise in this type of estimation is measuring secant lines, in an effort to estimate a tangent line. In studying a tangent line, you can apply this to the slope of a curve at one point. By measuring secant lines progressively closer to the tangent line you can estimate the tangent line. For a great animation of this go to *Secants and Tangents*.

Secants and Tangents
URL: http://www.math.psu.edu/dna/secants/secants1.mpg

3 For younger students, you could do a similar exercise using round objects and rulers. Ask the students to measure the diameter and the circumference of different objects, such as rolls of tape, jar lids, and shadows of balls. They can then mathematically find π for each circular object.

Exploring π

- Go to *Graphics for the Calculus Classroom*. Then travel to *Archimedes' calculation of* π and view the movie on the page.

  Graphics for the Calculus Classroom
  URL: http://www.math.psu.edu/dna/graphics.html

  Archimedes' calculation of π
  URL: http://www.math.psu.edu/dna/graphics.html#archimedes

- Then inscribe polygons inside circles. Increase the number of sides with each inscription. Assume that the radius of each circle is one and find the area of each polygon. Chart the areas of each polygon, and as you do, you will notice the relationship between the area of each polygon and the area of each circle.

Geometric Probability

Overview

For this lesson, your students explore simple probability and express probability geometrically.

Materials

- Graph paper
- Map or globe of the world

Objectives

- Represent simple probability geometrically using area of plane figures
- Count a random sample to determine the probability of an event occurring
- Calculate simple probability
- Work effectively in groups

Procedures

1 In this lesson, your students will be using challenge problems from *Math Magic*. Tell them to go to *Level 7–9, Cycle 1* under the menu Past Challenges and read the introduction to probability.

Math Magic
URL: http://forum.swarthmore.edu/mathmagic/

Level 7–9, Cycle 1
URL: ftp://forum.swarthmore.edu/mathmagic/7-9/cycle.001

❷ After your students gain basic knowledge of probability, ask them to practice drawing fractional parts of a plane figure's area on graph paper. Circles and rectangles work the best for easy calculation. Your students should work through the exercises in Cycle 1. They will be determining probability based on the fractional areas in the figure compared to the total area.

❸ Have your students apply this probability model to the workings of DNA. Ask them to go to the *Kids Corner* for background information on the DNA structure of mutating fruit flies for a good example of chance and probability in the real world.

Kid's Corner
URL: http://www.exploratorium.edu/learning_studio/lsxhibit.html

Mutant Fruit Fly
URL: http://www.exploratorium.edu/imagery/exhibits/mutant_flies/
       mutant_flies.html

❹ Have your students find the probability of each mutant type of fruit fly from the DNA structure. There are only four different chromosomes, so there would be a small amount of combinations. On their graph paper, have your students represent each mutant case as a fractional area of a plane figure.

🜚 Extensions

❶ Have your students break into groups of four. Give each group a bag of M&M's and graph paper. Each group will be responsible for counting the number of M&M's in each color and the total number of M&M's. From these numbers, your students can calculate the probability of drawing a certain color out of the bag of candy. This calculation is done for each color. Using the graph paper, your students now must draw a diagram that represents the probabilities of each color by area. The areas must be color coded. The area of each section must be equal to fraction of the total area that is its probability. At the end of the activity, let your students eat the M&M's.

❷ Have your students experiment with a deck of cards instead of candy. Have them represent different hands in geometric areas. For this extension, you can use *Math Magic Level 10–12, Cycle 16*. This site poses an extra question of a replacement or nonreplacement event.

Math Magic Level 10–12, Cycle 16
URL: ftp://forum.swarthmore.edu/mathmagic/10-12/cycle.016

Geometric Probability

- At the *Math Magic* site, go to *Level 7–9, Cycle 1* under the menu Past Challenges. Read the introduction to probability.

   Math Magic
   URL: http://forum.swarthmore.edu/mathmagic/

   Level 7–9, Cycle 1
   URL: ftp://forum.swarthmore.edu/mathmagic/7-9/cycle.001

- Go to the the *Kids Corner* for background information on the DNA structure of mutating fruit flies. Go to the *Mutant Fruit Fly* to find the probability of each mutant type of fruit fly.

   Kid's Corner
   URL: http://www.exploratorium.edu/learning_studio/lsxhibit.html

   Mutant Fruit Fly
   URL: http://www.exploratorium.edu/imagery/exhibits/mutant_flies/mutant_flies.html

It's the Method that Counts

Overview

This lesson shows students the step-by-step processes for solving problems using algorithms and the many applications of algorithms.

Materials

- Paper

Objectives

- Develop and apply strategies to solve a wide variety of problems
- Formulate problems from everyday situations
- Follow directions carefully and correctly

Procedures

1 Tell your students Math uses processes or procedures to solve problems. The abstract procedure, one without specific content, is the algorithm. Tell your students that today they will be using the algorithm to create a tour of a museum.

2 To begin, divide the class into groups of three. Then send your students to *Boston Museum of Science's Virtual Tour*. Ask each group to make a list of all of the sections in this exhibit.

Boston Museum of Science
URL: http://www.mos.org/

Boston Museum of Science's Virtual Tour
URL: http://www.mos.org/tour/tour1.html

❸ Now tell your students to begin writing their own tours. They will need to identify the steps in their tour, and they will need to arrange the steps in order from the beginning to the end. Remind them to create tours so easy to follow that someone with no knowledge of computers or of the museum will be able to follow the tours.

❹ After your students write their tours, ask them to exchange their work. Each group should check another group's tour. They should assess the tours for understandability, completeness, correctness, and creativity.

🜨 Extensions

❶ A good exercise in creating algorithms is programming robots. Since robots are not readily available, ask your students to pretend to be robots who have been programmed to perform certain tasks. Remind your "student robots" to perform no action without instruction.

❷ Tour other facilities on and offline, such as the *The Institute of Egyptian Art and Archeology*. Each time, increase the difficulty of the tour.

The Institute of Egyptian Art and Archeology
URL: http://www.memphis.edu/egypt/main.html

❸ Take your students on a trip by foot or by car. Have your students create the directions before you leave. This will be a good exercise in making algorithms and following directions. Perhaps you will find your students follow a lot of procedures, such as exiting the classroom, automatically.

It's the Method that Counts

- Go to *The Boston Museum of Science Virtual Tour*. With your group, make a list of all of the sections in this exhibit.

  Boston Museum of Science
  URL: http://www.mos.org/

  Boston Museum of Science's Virtual Tour
  URL: http://www.mos.org/tour/tour1.html

- Next, you and your group should write your own tour of the exhibit. Arrange the steps in your tour from the beginning to the end. Remember, you want to create a tour that will be understood by someone who isn't familiar with the workings of the heart or of computers. After you and your group finish, exchange your tour with another group. Take each other's tours, and assess them for understandability, completeness, correctness, and creativity.

Let's Paint!

 ## Objectives

- Use the Internet for research and information processing
- Measure perimeter, height, and area accurately
- Predict the amount of paint needed for a painting task
- Work effectively in teams
- Discover and utilize the formula for determining surface area

 ## Materials

- Measurement tools: yardstick, ruler, long tape measure
- Printer
- Graph paper (optional)

Procedures

1 Ask your students if they've ever helped their family or friends paint the interior of a house. Have they ever noticed that there is never enough paint, or even worse, too much paint that ends up on the curb with the rest of the refuse? Tell your students that accurate measuring and planning will help prevent this recurring painting nightmare from happening again.

2 Have your students divide into teams and peruse the school for possible rooms and area to paint a new, better color; students especially are very conscious of how awful that greying yellow ceiling over their lockers looks every day! Have each team choose a room or area of the school to "paint" and use their measuring tools to determine the perimeter of the floor, the height of the walls, and the area of the ceiling, and record the amount of doors and windows in their chosen area. Make sure your students take account of whether doors are double-doors, and the size of the windows. With this raw data, ask your students to predict the amount of paint they think will be necessary for this new "paint job" without computation: the way most of "us" do it!

3 Connect to the *Paint Estimator* site on the World Wide Web and enter the measured dimensions into the appropriate entry blocks to determine how much paint will be needed to finish the task. Consider how many coats of paint are necessary as well! Try to determine the formula for determining surface area from the computations the site makes with your inputted variables. See if any of your students' predictions were close. Discuss the possible causes of discrepancies between the actual amount and the predicted amount of paint.

Paint Estimator
URL: http://www.btw.com/applets/paint_calc.html

⚒ Extensions

1 Have your students use the same measurement activity for their room at home, their entire house, or they can research the dimensions of a famous building from reference material in your Media Center. Your students can figure out the amount of paint needed by using the formula for surface area, then they can bring in their answer and compare it with the amount that the *Paint Estimator* site returns. This time, look for mathematical discrepancies, not judgment errors.

2 Tour the photo and graphic exhibits at the *Architecture Database* to view a multitude of architectural wonders: from Frank Lloyd Wright to classical Mediterranean, and all for your students to search through, calculate the dimensions, and determine the amount of paint needed to "paint" them whichever horrible shade of chartreuse they can imagine!

Architecture Database

URL: http://rubens.anv.edu.au/architecture_form.html

❸ For a more challenging follow-up, connect to *The Virtual Study Tour* where you'll find virtual walkthroughs of famous architectural sites (not necessarily in dire need of a paint job) for your students to voyage through and determine the dimensions, and hence, the amount of paint needed to "improve" these works of architectural art. Students will have to keep a map on graph paper to maintain an accurate record of where they've stepped, and which direction they're facing on this virtual tour. Your students can also download videos of the walk-throughs if this activity becomes too challenging: you may find yourself getting lost in the mazes of rooms and corridors.

The Virtual Study Tour

URL: http://archpropplan.auckland.ac.nz/virtualtour/

❹ Your class could take part in an urban renewal project: find out if any of the older historic buildings in your town are dilapidated from lack of funds and manpower to renovate. Perhaps your class could assume a role in the gentrification of the building: from measuring and calcu-lating, to doing the actual painting or working with the architects to restore the natural beauty of the building.

Similar Triangles

Overview

The purpose of the lesson is to study similar triangles created from overlapping figures inscribed in circles and to show how similar triangles are used in real world situations.

Materials

- Graph Paper
- Paper
- Protractors and straight edges

Objectives

- Identify overlapping similar triangles
- Calculate the interior angles of triangles from given information
- Make conjectures from gathered information
- Create a definition from conjectures
- Use similar triangles to enlarge an object, keeping it the same shape

Procedures

1 In this lesson, your students will work with the diagrams from the *Find the Angles of the Vertices* off the Worksheet menu, in the *Geometry Center*.

Geometry Center
URL: http://forum.swarthmore.edu/~sarah/shapiro/shapiro/

Find the Angles of the Vertices
URL: http://forum.swarthmore.edu/~sarah/shapiro/shapiro/
    sum.angles.html.

❷ Tell your students to find five triangles from the top diagram that have the same shape but differ in size. These triangles will be the similar triangles. Ask your students to copy each triangle onto the graph paper, and to turn them so the triangles all have the same orientation. Caution your students to work carefully so the size of each triangle is preserved.

❸ Using the computer diagrams, ask your students to determine the interior angles of the chosen triangles. Tell your students to use the given information at the top of the page. Have the students label the interior angles in the corresponding triangles on the graph paper.

❹ Ask your students to repeat steps 2 and 3 for the middle and bottom diagrams, finding two and three similar triangles in each respectively.

❺ Your students now must make conjectures about the interior angles and other traits of similar triangles from their labeled sketches. From these conjectures, your students will create their own definitions of similar triangles.

❻ To apply these relationships, tell your students to look at the angles and triangles involved in origami, the ancient Japanese art of paper folding. From the models supplied here or others you might have, have the students practice folding by making some small origami objects.

❼ Unfold the origami creatures and have the students trace along the folds carefully with a pencil. Use protractors to measure the angles where folds meet. Transfer these angles to a much larger sheet of paper, being careful to place the angles correctly in the same corresponding position.

8 After all the angles are carefully transferred, connect the lines between vertex points. Fold the large sheet the same as the original origami object, now using the sketched lines as folds. The students should produce larger replicas of the same object. The similar triangles between the small and the large objects created similar origami final products.

✦ Extensions

1 If the students were given the radius of the circle (e.g., $r = 1$), they could calculate the length of each of the sides of the similar triangles. Then comparing the sides the students could determine the proportional nature of the sides of similar triangles.

2 Have your students study the similar angles and triangles within the inner structure of crystals growing in nature. Use a microscope to take a closer look. Grow your own crystals in the classroom. Have your students find agents that deter or damage this similar growing phenomenon.

3 Have your students study the way lenses use similar images to reduce or magnify objects. This can be tied to the inner working of the eye, cameras, or overhead projectors.

Cow's Eye Dissection
URL: http://www.exploratorium.edu/learning_studio/cow_eye/

4 Have your students study the importance of model building in architecture and development. Have them build exact miniature models of local buildings, or famous structures like the pyramids of Egypt. This is a huge application for the theory of similarity.

Similar Triangles

- At the *Geometry Through Art* site, work with the diagrams from the *Find the Angles of the Vertices* off the Worksheet Menu, in the *Geometry Center*.

  Geometry Center
  URL: http://forum.swarthmore.edu/~sarah/shapiro/shapiro/

  Find the Angles of the Vertices
  URL: http://forum.swarthmore.edu/~sarah/shapiro/shapiro/sum.angles.html.

Solving Word Problems

Overview

In this lesson, students become comfortable with the questions to ask and the steps to follow in solving Algebra word problems.

Materials

- Paper

Objectives

- Analyze the power of mathematical abstraction and symbolism
- Translate English phrases and sentences into mathematical expressions and equations.
- Solve word problems

Procedures

1 Since algebra requires your students to solve word problems, your students need to build a strong foundation of problem attack skills. To help them build these skills, send them to *21st Century Problem Solving*.

21st Century Problem Solving
URL: http://www2.hawaii.edu/suremath/home.shtml

2 Solving word problems is much like solving a puzzle. To solve either a puzzle or a word problem, you need to ask the correct questions in the correct sequence. This can be done by carefully reading the problem, asking the right questions, and considering the steps. To help your students develop these skills, send them to *Making Sense of Word Problems*. First ask them to look at the problems and to consider the questions to ask for solving the problems. After they've listed their questions, send them to this page.

Making Sense of Word Problems
URL: http://www2.hawaii.edu/suremath/
    story.problems.html#PROBLIST

3 Now ask your students to solve the word problems by using the methods they just studied at *Making Sense of Word Problems*. When they finish, send them to the *Interactive Problem Solving* page.

Interactive Problem Solving
URL: http://www2.hawaii.edu/suremath/page0Problem1.html

4 Now your students can create their own word problems by using techniques from the site. Remind them to create their problems by working backwards. They should start at the end of the problem and proceed to the beginning. For ideas on working backwards, have your students look at these examples in *Algebra Story Problems*.

Algebra Story Problems
URL: http://www2.hawaii.edu/suremath/intro_algebra.html

🜔 Extensions

1 Physics shows how problem-solving applies to the real world. To show your students why learning how to solve problems is so valuable, send them to the *Physics Problems* site.

Physics Problems
URL: http://www2.hawaii.edu/suremath/physicsProblems.html

2 For more advanced problem solving techniques, bring the methods at this site into your Chemistry class.

Chemistry Problems
URL: http://www2.hawaii.edu/suremath/chemistryProblems.html

3 As a treat on a nice day, ask your students to grab their notebooks and run outside to the track. When you are at the track, give your students distance word problems to solve. Be sure they record all their data before returning to the classroom.

Solving Word Problems

- To build your word problem-solving skills, go to *21st Century Problem Solving*.

  21st Century Problem Solving
  URL: http://www2.hawaii.edu/suremath/home.shtml

- Now go to *Making Sense of Word Problems*. Look at the problems and consider the questions to ask for solving them.

  Making Sense of Word Problems
  URL: http://www2.hawaii.edu/suremath/story.problems.html#PROBLIST

- Solve the problems using the methods described. When you finish, go to the *Interactive Problem Solving* page.

  Interactive Problem Solving
  URL: http://www2.hawaii.edu/suremath/page0Problem1.html

- Now create your own word problems by starting at the end of the problem and working to the beginning. For ideas on working backwards, look at these examples in *Algebra Story Problems*.

  Algebra Story Problems
  URL: http://www2.hawaii.edu/suremath/intro_algebra.html

Science

Lesson Plans,

Activity Sheets,

and Student Handouts

A Note on the Organization

Lesson plans are arranged in alphabetical order, with grade levels indicated in the top left corner.

Student handouts are included with some of the lesson plans and are identified with a computer icon on the top left-hand corner.

Stand-alone activity sheets appear at the end of the chapter.

Acceleration and the Earth's Gravity

Overview

In this lesson, your students will recreate Galileo's experiment for finding the acceleration due to gravity.

Materials

- Ramps (2 meters long)
- Wooden blocks
- "Hot Wheels" tracks
- Stopwatches
- Balls
- Tape

Objectives

- Collect and categorize data
- Develop scientific skills

Procedures

1 Tell your students that Aristotle, a leader in the scientific community even during his lifetime, (384–322 B.C.), believed that when two objects are thrown from the same height, the heavier object will reach the ground before the lighter object. Centuries later, the Italian astronomer and physicist, Galileo took the study of gravity further. Galileo, who lived from 1564 to 1642, argued that both objects would reach the ground at the same time, because gravity exerts the same force on all objects.

❷ Instruct your students to proceed to *The Art of Renaissance Science*. Ask them to read the introductory chapter entitled *Galileo* portraying Galileo's life and contributions. Tell your students to imagine themselves back in Galileo's time. Often the sciences are conveyed to students as dry facts from nameless, faceless books, but remind your students that real people, like themselves, make the discoveries in experimental science.

The Art of Renaissance Science
URL: http://bang.lanl.gov/video/stv/arshtml/lanlarstitle.html

Galileo
URL: http://bang.lanl.gov/video/stv/arshtml/galileo1.html

❸ Now your students are going to discover the constancy of gravity for themselves. Measuring moving bodies in free fall is difficult because the bodies move so fast, but Galileo devised an experiment to make measuring gravity much easier. He rolled a ball down a slope to measure the effects of gravity in a slower context. While the force acting on the ball rolling down the slope is just a fraction of the force of gravity, it still demonstrates that the force of gravity works the same on all objects. No matter how the experiment is done and what size the objects, the force of gravity working on them is the same.

❹ Instruct your students to read the page *Galileo and the Mathematics of Motion Part I*, which shows the tools and techniques Galileo used to study gravity and the details of his experiment. Be sure they watch the animations and take notes for the experiments they're about to do. Tell them to be ready to compare Galileo's experiment to their own.

Galileo and the Mathematics of Motion Part I: The Inclined Plane Experiments
URL: http://bang.lanl.gov/video/stv/arshtml/mathofmotion1.html

Now your students should set up their ramp:

❺ Arrange the ramp so the angle of the incline is at about 30° with respect to the table top. Place the "Hot Wheels" track on top of the ramp. Put a wooden block or book at the "finish" line to stop the ball from rolling off the ramp.

6 Measure from the top of the track about 20 cm and draw a zero line. Place tape marks at 10 cm, 40 cm, 90 cm, and 160 cm measured down from the zero line.

7 Have your students use a ruler or pencil to hold the ball at its starting position. Now have them quickly remove the ruler or pencil to release the ball. Using a stopwatch, have your students measure the time it takes the ball to cover the various distances.

8 Now have your students complete the accompanying chart to find the acceleration due to gravity. Your students will perform three time trials to measure the time the ball takes to reach each mark. They will be measuring the ball 12 times. Then they will use this data to complete the chart. Try not to give them all the information they need to figure acceleration due to gravity, the final column of their chart. Instead, tell them to read about Galileo's experiment for putting the relationship puzzle together. Your students will finally realize each acceleration should be the same because gravity works the same on all objects.

✿ Extensions

1 You can perform a similar experiment to directly measure the acceleration due to gravity with free falling bodies. Have your students drop an object from shoulder-height. Then measure the time the object took to fall and the distance it traveled. For a movie and an explanation of free falling bodies, send your students to Galileo Part I: The Early Years.

Galileo Part I: The Early Years
URL: http://bang.lanl.gov/video/stv/arshtml/galileo1.html

2 Now have your students drop two objects of different weights from shoulder-height. Ask your students to notice which one hits first. The heavier one like Aristotle said, or do they hit at the same time like Galileo said? Your students will realize, despite the different weights of the objects, that the objects hit, just like Galileo argued, at the same time. Gravity exerts the same force on all objects.

3 As closure to this lesson, and if your students have had some algebra, have them derive the standard formula that involves distance, time, and acceleration. You supply the formulas that they used in the experiment, and ask your students to derive the acceleration formula.

The acceleration formula: $d = \dfrac{at^2}{2}$

The formulas your students can use to derive this formula:

    i) $\dfrac{d}{t}$ = average speed

    ii) $\text{speed}_{(final)} + \text{speed}_{(initial)}/2$ = average speed

    iii) $2 \times (\text{average speed}) - \text{speed}_{(initial)} = \text{speed}_{(final)}$

    iv) $(\text{speed}_{(final)} - \text{speed}_{(initial)})/t = \text{acceleration}$

Acceleration and the Earth's Gravity

- Read the introductory chapter entitled *Galileo* at *The Art of Renaissance Science*, and try to imagine yourself back in Galileo's time. Often the sciences are conveyed as dry facts from nameless, faceless books, but real people like yourself make the discoveries in experimental science.

  The Art of Renaissance Science
  URL: http://bang.lanl.gov/video/stv/arshtml/lanlarstitle.html

  Galileo
  URL: http://bang.lanl.gov/video/stv/arshtml/galileo1.html

- Now you are going to discover the constancy of gravity for yourself. Read the page *Galileo and the Mathematics of Motion Part I*, which shows the tools and techniques Galileo used to study gravity and the details of his experiment. Be sure to watch the animations and take notes for the experiment you're about to do. Be ready to compare Galileo's experiment to your own.

  Galileo and the Mathematics of Motion Part I: The Inclined Plane Experiments
  URL: http://bang.lanl.gov/video/stv/arshtml/mathofmotion1.html

- Now set up the ramp:
  a. Arrange the ramp so the angle of the incline is at about 30° with respect to the table top. Put the "Hot Wheels" track on top of the ramp. Place a wooden block or book at the "finish" line to stop the ball from rolling off the ramp.

  b. Measure from the top of the track about 20 cm and draw a zero line. Place tape marks at 10 cm, 40 cm, 90 cm, and 160 cm measured down from the zero line.

  c. Use a ruler or pencil to hold the ball at its starting position. Quickly pull it away to release the ball. Using a stopwatch, measure the time it takes the ball to cover the various distances.

- Now complete the accompanying chart to find the acceleration due to gravity. You will perform three time trials to measure the time the ball takes to reach each mark. You will be measuring the ball 12 times and using the data to fill out the chart.

The Great Sharks
Misunderstood and On Trial!

Overview

- Use research skills
- Use the Internet to research information on sharks
- Deliberate, thorough proof, facts from myths about sharks

Materials

- Color printer
- Blackboard or overhead projector

Procedures

1 Open up a class discussion with the prompt: "The last time you were at the beach, basking in the warm sun, cooling off in the refreshing water, what was the worst thing you imagined could happen to you?" Allow your students to contribute their responses until someone says: "Get eaten by a giant shark, like in Jaws!" From this point, brainstorm with your class all facts and opinions regarding sharks and record the data on the blackboard. Divide the blackboard up in half; ask your students to vote on each point: either it is fact or myth. Gather as many thoughts on sharks as possible: at least 20.

2 Connect to the *Marine Biology Database* and allow your students to research the background information on sharks. Your students will choose from many forms of marine life on this list; make sure they view at least five of the shark selections on this site. View and print the graphic images of the sharks. Use the information found here to clarify some of the fact/myths about sharks. Keep a record of the facts and myths current on the board as students find the answers.

Marine Biology Database
URL: http://www.calpoly.edu:80/delta.html

3 Connect to the *Mote Marine Laboratory* site for a humorous and informative look at common shark myths. This site will supplant the basic information gained from the Marine Biology Database, and your students will probe more deeply into myths about sharks. Again, record the facts/myths on the board as they are deliberated by your students.

Shark Pages: Mote Marine Laboratory
URL: http://www.marinelab.sarasota.fl.us/~rhueter/sharks/shark.phtml

4 For even more information on popular shark myths and misconceptions, connect to the *Beyond Jaws* site and let your students read on about the reality of sharks. All these sites contain graphics and text that can be downloaded, printed, and used for "evidence" in deciding whether the point is fact or myth. Allow your student groups to search for clues about each point on their own; this will lend an air of "friendly competition" to your lesson, as well as make students feel they are "scientific super-sleuths" in search of the truth.

Beyond Jaws
URL: http://hockey.plaidworks.com:80/sharks/great-white.html

5 If your list is still incomplete after the lesson, suggest further online research. If any of your unresolved points about sharks pertain to the history of the shark, connect to the *Finding an Expert Online* site and follow the link from Ask a Paleontologist to the UCMP Berkeley site, where you can email your questions to an actual paleontologist! This should help your class and you "flesh out" your list.

Finding an Expert Online
URL: http://www.fwl.org:80/edtech/experts.html

72

Lesson Plan   The Great Sharks: Misunderstood and On Trial!
··
Teaching Grades K–12 with the Internet

⬛ Extensions

❶ Research the *Fishopedia* for more information on sharks from the sport-fisherman's point of view. Compare the information listed (or deleted) here to sites you've explored in your lesson. What topics and special considerations are made by fishermen that are not covered by scientists, and vice versa. Why do you think there is a difference?

Fishopedia
URL: http://calfish/fishop.thm

❷ You can lead your class to an interactive journey through the *Prehistoric Shark Museum* to discover more about the history of sharks. This site is rich with graphics and links to other shark-related sites on the Internet.

Prehistoric Shark Museum
URL: http://emporium.turnpike.net/C/celestial/epsm.htm

❸ View images of sharks and their favorite prey at the *Shark Images* site.

Shark Images
URL: http://www.ucmp.berkeley.edu/vertebrates/Doug/shark.html

❹ Post an email message to the surfer Usenet Newsgroup alt.surfing asking for information, personal accounts, folklore, etc. about sharks. Some surfers have a more intimate relationship with sharks than do scientists! Read through the posts ahead of time so you can find and print out the messages and threads of ongoing discussions of sharks. There are always "experts" online waiting to share their real-life shark stories. Surfers from over the globe come into contact with sharks every day in the water.

Surfer Usenet Newsgroup
URL: news:alt.surfing

Lab Lightning

Overview

In this lesson, students will discover the basics of static electricity by creating static electricity in the classroom.

Materials

- Two swatches of nylon material for every student
- A bag of balloons for every three students in your class
- Carpet samples, if your room is uncarpeted

Objectives

- Examine matter and energy through static electricity
- Discover the structure and characteristics of static electricity
- Recognize the natural and man-made causes of static electricity

Procedures

❶ To begin the study of static electricity, ask your students to share their experiences with electricity. Have they ever received an electric shock? How did it happen? Do they know why? Now take your students to the *Boston Museum of Science* and its *Theater of Electricity*.

Boston Museum of Science
URL: http://www.mos.org/

Theater of Electricity

URL: http://www.mos.org/sln/toe/toe.html

2 For the basics of electricity, travel with your students to the *Sparks* section for information about voltage, charge, conductivity, and insulation. Show them the attached glossary of science terms, and ask them to use the glossary to list and define voltage, charge, conductivity and insulation.

Sparks

URL: http://www.mos.org/sln/toe/sparks.html

Science Glossary

URL: http://www.mos.org/sln/toe/glossary.html

3 Now have your students experience static electricity safely. Divide your students into groups of three, and give each group six pieces of nylon fabric and one bag of balloons. Have each group blow up their balloons, while you make the classroom as dark as possible. After the students finish blowing up their balloons, have each person briskly rub two pieces of nylon fabric together. This will create static electricity. In the dark, your students should see the sparks and perhaps hear the snap of the electric charges jumping back and forth as they rub the nylon pieces.

As your students continue to rub the nylon fabric back and forth, tell your students to rub their feet on the carpet. Ask them to almost, but not quite, touch metal objects. Your students should experience mild, but safe shocks.

4 Now tell your class their groups are about to compete in an unusual balloon race. Each group will be using static electricity to get balloons to cling to a student, and the group with the most balloons clinging to a student wins. Ask each group to find one member willing to be electrically charged in a safe and painless way. The volunteers for each group should stand quietly while the other two students in the group rub the person with nylon swatches and carpet. After the volunteers have been electrically charged, the students should attach the balloons. How many balloons can each group get to cling to their volunteer?

❺ To show your students more ways static electricity can be produced, take your students to these three Van de Graaff Generator sites.

History of the Van de Graaff Generator
URL: http://www.mos.org/sln/toe/history.html

Construction of the Van de Graaff Generator
URL: http://www.mos.org/sln/toe/construction.html

Movie of the Van de Graaff Generator
URL: http://www.mos.org/sln/toe/VDG_works.mov

⚙ Extensions

❶ Have your students explore the natural phenomenon of static electricity, lightning. Go to *Lightning* in the *Museum of Science* for diagrams and pictures.

Lightning
URL: http://www.mos.org/sln/toe/lightning.html

❷ What should you do when you're caught outside in a sudden thunderstorm? To find out, have your students take the *Lightning Safety Quiz*.

Lightning Safety Quiz
URL: http://www.mos.org/sln/toe/safety.html

❸ For another experiment with static electricity, have your students experiment with more materials to see which ones produce static electricity. For example, a plastic rod and a swatch of fur, or a balloon and a swatch of wool, are pairs of materials that produce static electricity after being rubbed together.

Lab Lightning

- After you've discussed static electricity in class with your teacher, go to the *Boston Museum of Science* and its *Theater of Electricity*.

  Boston Museum of Science
  URL: http://www.mos.org/

  Theater of Electricity
  URL: http://www.mos.org/sln/toe/toe.html

- Now travel to the *Sparks* section for information about voltage, charge, conductivity, and insulation. Use the attached glossary to list and define voltage, charge, conductivity, and insulation.

  Sparks
  URL: http://www.mos.org/sln/toe/sparks.html

  Science Glossary
  URL: http://www.mos.org/sln/toe/glossary.html

- After you've completed your in-class experiments with static electricity, go with your students to these three Van de Graaff Generator sites. They will show you more ways static electricity can be produced, and don't miss the movie!

  History of the Van de Graaff Generator
  URL: http://www.mos.org/sln/toe/history.html

  Construction of the Van de Graaff Generator
  URL: http://www.mos.org/sln/toe/construction.html

  Movie of the Van de Graaff Generator
  URL: http://www.mos.org/sln/toe/VDG_works.mov

Microscope

Find the Pictures

Overview

In this lesson, your students will be exploring the purpose and use of microscopes.

Materials

- Computer with Internet access
- Magnifying glasses
- Books with hidden pictures such as titles in the *Where's Waldo* series
- Paper, pencil
- Microscope

Objectives

- Examine and describe scientific images
- Express how scientific images can be compared to each other
- Explore simple magnifying devices and the concepts behind them

Procedures

1 Give your students magnifying glasses and picture books featuring tiny pictures hidden within larger ones, such as *Where's Waldo*. Or, send your students to the find the five hidden dinosaurs at the *Questacon* site.

Questacon Kidspace
URL http://sunsite.anu.edu.au/Questacon/kidspace/ksspot.html

Ask your students to search for the hidden pictures using the magnifying glasses. After they have found the hidden pictures with their magnifying glasses, tell them that microscopes see even more than magnifying glasses. Tell them microscopes see the part of the world that is invisible to our eyes.

2 Now show your students what kind of pictures they can see with a microscope. Go to the online exhibition about the microscope called *Scanning Electron Microscope* at the *Boston Museum of Science*. Ask your students how these pictures look different from what they saw with their magnifying glasses. Ask them how the pictures of the invisible world seen by the microscope and the world seen by the human eye compare.

Boston Museum of Science
URL: http://www.mos.org/

Scanning Electron Microscope
URL: http://www.mos.org/sln/sem/intro.html

3 Tell them to choose four pictures at *Scanning Electron Microscope* and to write a short description about each of the four.

4 Next, have your students look at tiny, everyday objects, such as a bit of pencil, paper or chalk, with their magnifying glasses. Finally, have them take a look at the same objects under a microscope. Talk about the differences between what they can see with their naked eye, a magnifying glass, and a microscope.

⚡ Extensions

1 Have your students sketch an everyday object as seen under a magnifying glass or microscope. Tell them to pay particular attention to the textures. For close-ups of objects showing textures, look at the *Scanning Electron Microscope* page.

Scanning Electron Microscope
URL: http://www.mos.org/sln/sem/intro.html

② For your students to get an idea of the internal workings of matter you can send them to *Chemistry Visualized*. At this site are animations of atoms moving as you could see if you had a powerful microscope. You can explore structure of molecules and atoms.

Chemistry Visualized
URL: http://www-wilson.ucsd.edu/education/samplegateway.html

③ For a great continuation of this lesson, travel to the *ION Science News* article titled *Computers See Deep into the Structure of Life*. This article focuses on how computers today are helping microscopes become much clearer in their imaging. The computers take the microscope image, run it through a program, and come out with a clear picture from a blurry image. Your students will love learning about these computers.

Computers See Deep into the Structure of Life
URL: http://njw.injersey.com/media/IonSci/glance/news795/
microsco.html

ION Science News
URL: http://njw.injersey.com/media/IonSci/

Microscope
Find the Pictures

- Using the magnifying glass your teacher has given you, find the five hidden dinosaurs at this page on the *Questacon* site.

  Questacon Kidspace
  URL: http://sunsite.anu.edu.au/Questacon/kidspace/ksspot.html

- You saw how magnifying glasses helped you to find hidden pictures. Now you will see how microscopes help you see things so tiny you can't even see them with a magnifying glass. Go to the online exhibition about the microscope called *Scanning Electron Microscope* at the *Boston Museum of Science*.

  Boston Museum of Science
  URL: http://www.mos.org/

  Scanning Electron Microscope
  URL: http://www.mos.org/sln/sem/intro.html

- How are these pictures different from what you saw with a magnifying glass?

Tour the Circulatory System

Overview

The purpose of this lesson is for students to explore the circulatory system, its parts, and the functions it performs in keeping the body healthy.

Materials

- None

 Objectives

- Describe the structures and functions of the human body's circulatory system.
- Describe the structures and functions of the blood vessels in the human body's circulatory system.
- Express the functional relationships between the various parts of the human body's circulatory system.

Procedures

1 Take your students to the Franklin Institute's *The Heart: An Online Exploration*. They should go to the *Circulatory System*.

The Heart: An Online Exploration
URL: http://sln2.fi.edu/biosci/heart.html

Circulatory System
URL: http://sln2.fi.edu/biosci/systems/circulation.html

2 Your students will spend time at this page becoming familiar with the three main parts of the circulatory system. They should note the functions of each, as well as the function of the encompassing circulatory system.

3 Your students will now go to *Blood Vessels*. After exploring the larger systems, your students will now explore the means in which these systems function. At this point your students become familiar with arteries,veins, and capillaries.

Blood Vessels
URL: http://sln2.fi.edu/biosci/vessels/vessels.html

4 Make your students travel down an artery, viewing the movie located at Trip Down a Coronary Artery. After touring this section of the exhibit, your students should be able to explain what happens at the end of the movie.

Trip Down a Coronary Artery
URL: http://www.mco.edu/iarc/movies/coronary.mov

Extensions

1 A great activity is to explore the inner workings of human blood at *Lifeblood*. These pages go into great depth into the structure and function of this "fascinating fluid of life."

Lifeblood
URL: http://sln2.fi.edu/biosci/blood/blood.html

2 Explore the heart in great detail at *The Heart: An Online Exploration*. For those students whom do not upset easily, view the movie of open heart surgery at *Take a Look Inside*. Also get an in-depth explanation of the workings of an artificial heart at Building a Better Heart.

Take a Look Inside
URL: http://sln2.fi.edu/biosci/healthy/openheart.html

Building a Better Heart
URL: http://sln2.fi.edu/biosci/healthy/fake.html

❸ Have your students participate in the *HeartBeat Activity*. Show your students the way doctors used to listen to the heart. This method is the way doctors discovered ways of caring for the heart.

HeartBeat Activity

URL: http://sln2.fi.edu/biosci/activity/bio-2.html

❹ You can spend quality class time having your students explore the techniques of keeping a heart healthy. There are excellent pages dealing with diet, exercise, blood pressure, and drugs. You can start at *A Prescription for Living*.

A Prescription for Living

URL: http://sln2.fi.edu/biosci/healthy/healthy.html

We Love Cockroaches!

Overview

The purpose of this lesson is to explore the cockroach, not as a pest, but as a fellow organism on this planet. The goal is to discover how much we have in common with the cockroach.

Materials

- Computer with Internet access
- Paper

Objectives

- Compare and contrast characteristics of cockroaches and humans.
- Describe the basic needs of an organism (for example, food, water, air, shelter, space)
- Recognize a similarity in the basic needs of living organisms and how they affect their own environment.

Procedures

1 Begin by proceeding to *Cockroach World*. Your students should begin to browse through *A Day in the Life of Rodney Roach* in *Cockroach World*.

Cockroach World
URL: http://www.nj.com/yucky/roaches/index.html

A Day in the Life of Rodney Roach
URL: http://www.nj.com/yucky/life/index.html

❷ Have your students follow Rodney Roach's day. Then have the students make a list of the basic needs of a roach and a list of the basic needs of a human. Your students will then compare lists and draw any conclusions; noting any similarities or differences.

❸ Your students will now proceed to *The Inside Story* at *Cockroach World*. Looking at the dissection of the cockroach, have the students make a chart of body parts in common and those not in common.

The Inside Story
URL: http://www.nj.com/yucky/inside/index.html

❹ Finally, discuss with your students the findings from their comparing and contrasting exercise. They should recognize that even though there are differences, there are a lot of things we have in common. To show complete understanding the students should be able to relate this relationship to being fellow organisms sharing this planet.

Extensions

❶ For fun and excitement have your students go to *How to Catch Big Cockroaches*. Proceed through the steps to make a cockroach trap for home.

After the students have their own cockroach to study, they can learn much more about the cockroach.

How to Catch Big Cockroaches
URL: http://www.nj.com/yucky/journal/index.html

❷ For a marvelously entertaining lesson have your students go to *Cockroach Love* in *ION Science*. Explore pheromones and the behavior they cause.

ION Science
URL: http://njw.injersey.com/media/IonSci/

Cockroach Love
URL: http://njw.injersey.com/media/IonSci/features/roach/
roach.html

3 For further study, invite a local exterminator, entomologist, or health professional into your classroom to answer questions your students might have. They could give valuable insights into catching and controlling cockroach problems. You could discuss the health concerns involving cockroaches.

4 You can do similar lessons involving other insects. You can compare insects. For example, you can compare moths to butterflies. You can do an in-depth study into the worm. For invaluable information on worms travel to *Worm World*.

Worm World
URL: http://www.nj.com/yucky/worm/index.html

5 For global comprehension, have your students locate cockroach habitats on a world map. They can color in different spots using different colors for different climates. For an interactive activity showing different cockroach locations around the world go to *Around the World with a Cockroach* in *Cockroach World*.

Cockroach World
URL: http://www.nj.com/yucky/roaches/index.html

Around the World with a Cockroach
URL: http://www.nj.com/yucky/world/index.html

6 If your students are demanding more insect sites, consider bees. *B-EYE* is a site devoted to the study of bees. For an excellent activity, have your students look at the site's special feature, viewing pictures as a bee would see them.

B-EYE: The world through the eyes of a bee
URL: http://cvs.anu.edu.au/andy/beye/beyehome.html

7 For further study of all types of creepy critters, take your students to *Minibeast World*. This site has teacher and student resources along with conservation and environmental activities.

Minibeast World of Insects and Spiders
URL: http://www.tesser.com/minibeast/

8 For in-depth study of insects, take your students to the *Department of Entomology* at *Iowa State University*. This site offers great insect graphics, links to the hottest Insect research sites and interactive activities.

Department of Entomology—ISU
URL: http://www.public.iastate.edu/~entomology/

Worms, Nature's Recyclers

Overview

In this lesson, your students will build a worm bin to discover how worms help the environment by recycling garbage.

Materials

- 2 pieces ⅝" CDX plywood (35⅜" × 12")
  [*Note:* CDX is a special type of wood.]
- 2 pieces ⅝" CDX plywood (23⅜" × 12")
- 1 piece ⅝" CDX plywood (24" × 36")
- 38 2" ardox nails, hammer, drill with ½" bit
- Worms
- Soil
- Garbage from the school cafeteria

Objectives

- Study the behavior and basic needs of an organism, in particular, the worm
- Discover the ecological benefits of recycling
- Experience the responsibility of caring for living things

Procedures

❶ To begin this exciting lesson, take your students to *Worm World* at *The Yuckiest Site*. You and your class will build and maintain a worm bin as a class project. You can conduct this project in as little as one week, or you can choose to continue it throughout the school year. But since this is a class project, you will only need enough materials to make one worm bin.

The Yuckiest Site
URL: http://www.nj.com/yucky/

Worm World
URL: http://www.nj.com/yucky/worm/index.html

❷ Focus your students' attention on the *Worms as Recyclers* page, where they will discover how worms recycle and what they recycle. Tell your students that since worms help the environment, your class will be helping the environment by recycling school garbage in the worm bin you will construct.

Worms as Recyclers
URL: http://www.nj.com/yucky/worm/recyclers/index.html

❸ Now you can build your worm bin and start recycling some of the garbage from your school cafeteria. Follow the directions at the *Make Your Own Worm Bin* page.

Make Your Own Worm Bin
URL: http://www.nj.com/yucky/worm/recyclers/howto.html

⊞ Extensions

❶ If you teach older students, take them to the *Body Parts* page for a virtual dissection. Have them watch the dissection images and interactive movies. They can write lab reports as if they had dissected worms, or you can use these pages as preparation for worm dissections.

Body Parts
URL: http://www.nj.com/yucky/worm/body/index.html

❷ Turn your adventure with worms into a language arts activity. First have your students read the poems in the *Worm Poetry Corner*. Then have them write their own worm poetry. Just make sure they write from the perspective of the worm!

Worm Poetry Corner
URL: http://www.nj.com/yucky/worm/gallery/poetry.html

❸ For an in-depth study of the reproductive cycle of the worm, send your students to the *Multimedia Room* in *Worm World*. After they hear the Worm Lady and watch a movie of a worm being hatched, have them make a list of the ten most surprising facts about worms.

Multimedia Room
URL: http://www.nj.com/yucky/worm/multi/index.html

Worms, Nature's Recyclers

- You're about to discover how worms help our environment. At *The Yuckiest Site*, go to *Worm World* and *Worms as Recyclers*.

  The Yuckiest Site
  URL: http://www.nj.com/yucky/

  Worm World
  URL: http://www.nj.com/yucky/worm/index.html

  Worms as Recyclers
  URL: http://www.nj.com/yucky/worm/recyclers/index.html

- You and your class will be building a worm bin to help your school recycle its cafeteria garbage. Follow the directions at the *Make Your Own Worm Bin*.

  Make Your Own Worm Bin
  URL: http://www.nj.com/yucky/worm/recyclers/howto.html

Meteor Puzzle

Student name:_____

Step	A	Find the words that answer the clues, then find those words in the word search on the next page.

Step	B	All the information you will need is located within the Heavenly Fireworks story in the ION Science News.

Heavenly Fireworks

URL: http://njw.injersey.com/media/IonSci/features/perseids/perseids.html

ION Science News

URL: http://njw.injersey.com/media/IonSci/

1. These are like dirty snowballs. _____

2. Pieces of space debris ranging from microscopic to baseball size. _____

3. Pieces of space debris that hit the ground. _____

4. The path which an object travels around the sun. _____

5. A comet's tail always points away from this. _____

6. When this crosses a comet's path, the result is an increase in the amount of meteors we see. _____

7. This is formed by solar wind pushing away gas and dust. _____

8. The cloud of dust that is formed when the sun melts a comet's icy core. _____

9. The answer to question 8 is also called this. _____

10. Large meteors that splatter when they hit our atmosphere. _____

11. The annual meteor shower we can see in late summer. _____

12. The point in the sky where a meteor shower will emerge from. _____

13. The best time to view the Perseids is from _____ to _____.

14. The three major compounds that form a comet. _____

15. The Perseids will appear between these two bodies in the night sky. _____

16. This is what we actually see vaporizing when we see a meteor. _____

Meteor Puzzle
(continued)

Student name:

V	W	N	O	J	E	D	R	I	P	O	W	F	R	G	V	A	O	Q	S
C	C	D	N	U	T	O	D	W	O	R	V	U	P	X	Q	A	V	R	I
Q	L	K	H	V	I	M	F	S	V	F	B	S	Q	E	S	Z	K	G	L
L	Q	J	I	A	R	X	I	I	V	E	G	K	I	A	C	M	V	F	A
W	I	Y	V	P	O	A	G	D	U	R	Q	Q	A	G	J	G	U	A	R
S	I	A	K	C	E	E	O	P	N	Q	F	K	M	M	C	N	L	U	A
C	P	Y	T	U	T	M	M	X	U	I	G	S	B	D	F	K	M	Y	P
E	A	R	P	T	E	H	T	R	A	E	G	S	E	M	X	K	K	L	O
N	X	R	V	G	M	N	W	A	D	Q	G	H	L	F	F	W	X	R	L
A	V	N	B	Y	B	E	H	X	Z	J	R	Y	T	Q	K	O	Y	S	E
H	K	I	D	O	T	E	M	O	C	R	Z	E	U	Z	E	J	D	K	M
T	I	Z	A	A	N	X	R	A	E	X	L	L	A	B	E	R	I	F	A
E	M	D	M	N	L	D	E	O	D	N	T	D	A	E	H	G	K	J	C
M	K	K	O	U	X	V	I	H	E	E	D	I	W	B	H	R	C	T	W
L	I	X	C	S	O	U	O	O	R	T	J	R	B	S	I	R	B	E	D
T	N	A	I	D	A	R	W	A	X	O	E	V	S	R	U	V	K	J	D
P	E	R	S	E	I	D	Y	G	C	I	D	M	A	E	O	L	D	E	W
L	F	C	P	D	B	M	A	P	F	Y	D	A	I	N	O	M	M	A	W
T	H	L	S	N	X	M	L	H	J	O	U	E	P	E	R	S	E	U	S
W	S	X	O	W	W	N	R	O	D	V	J	Y	E	Q	H	O	S	A	L

Activity Sheet   Meteor Puzzle

Meteor Puzzle

Answer Key

| Step | A | Find the words that answer the clues, then find those words in the word search on the next page. |

| Step | B | All the information you will need is located within the Heavenly Fireworks story in the ION Science News. |

Heavenly Fireworks

URL: http://njw.injersey.com/media/IonSci/features/perseids/perseids.html

ION Science News

URL: http://njw.injersey.com/media/IonSci/

ANSWER KEY

1. These are like dirty snowballs. . . . . **COMET**
2. Pieces of space debris ranging from microscopic to baseball size. . . . . **METEOR**
3. Pieces of space debris that hit the ground. . . . . **METEORITE**
4. The path which an object travels around the sun. . . . . **ORBIT**
5. A comet's tail always points away from this. . . . . **SUN**
6. When this crosses a comet's path, the result is an increase in the amount of meteor's we see. . . . . **EARTH**
7. This is formed by solar wind pushing away gas and dust. . . . . **TAIL**
8. The cloud of dust that is formed when the sun melts a comet's icy core. . . . . **HEAD**
9. The answer to question 8 is also called this. . . . . **COMA**
10. Large meteors that splatter when they hit our atmosphere. . . . . **FIREBALL**
11. The annual meteor shower we can see in late summer. . . . . **PERSEID**
12. The point in the sky where a meteor shower will emerge from. . . . . **RADIANT**
13. The best time to view the Perseids is from . . . . **MIDNIGHT** to **DAWN**
14. The three major compounds that form a comet. . . . . **CARBON DIOXIDE, AMMONIA, METHANE**
15. The Perseids will appear between these two bodies in the night sky. . . . . **PERSEUS, CAMELOPARALIS**
16. This is what we actually see vaporizing when we see a meteor. . . . . **DEBRIS**

Meteor Puzzle

Answer Key (continued)

Student name: _____

V	W	N	O	J	E	D	R	I	P	O	W	F	R	G	V	A	O	Q	S
C	C	D	N	U	T	O	D	W	O	R	V	U	P	X	Q	A	V	R	I
Q	L	K	H	V	I	M	F	S	V	F	B	S	Q	E	S	Z	K	G	L
L	Q	J	I	A	R	X	I	I	V	E	G	K	I	A	C	M	V	F	A
W	I	Y	V	P	O	A	G	D	U	R	Q	Q	A	G	J	G	U	A	R
S	I	A	K	C	E	E	O	P	N	Q	F	K	M	M	C	N	L	U	A
C	P	Y	T	U	T	M	M	X	U	I	G	S	B	D	F	K	M	Y	P
E	A	R	P	T	E	H	T	R	A	E	G	S	E	M	X	K	K	L	O
N	X	R	V	G	M	N	W	A	D	Q	G	H	L	F	F	W	X	R	L
A	V	N	B	Y	B	E	H	X	Z	J	R	Y	T	Q	K	O	Y	S	E
H	K	I	D	O	T	E	M	O	C	R	Z	E	U	Z	E	J	D	K	M
T	I	Z	A	A	N	X	R	A	E	X	L	L	A	B	E	R	I	F	A
E	M	D	M	N	L	D	E	O	D	N	T	D	A	E	H	G	K	J	C
M	K	K	O	U	X	V	I	H	E	E	D	I	W	B	H	R	C	T	W
L	I	X	C	S	O	U	O	O	R	T	J	R	B	S	I	R	B	E	D
T	N	A	I	D	A	R	W	A	X	O	E	V	S	R	U	V	K	J	D
P	E	R	S	E	I	D	Y	G	C	I	D	M	A	E	O	L	D	E	W
L	F	C	P	D	B	M	A	P	F	Y	D	A	I	N	O	M	M	A	W
T	H	L	S	N	X	M	L	H	J	O	U	E	P	E	R	S	E	U	S
W	S	X	O	W	W	N	R	O	D	V	J	Y	E	Q	H	O	S	A	L

Surviving a Lunar Crash

Student name: _____

Step A

You are a member of a lunar flight scheduled to land at an established base on the moon. Due to mechanical difficulties, you and your partner are forced to land approximately 400 kilometers from the base. During the landing, most of your equipment is damaged, but you and your partner still have your spacesuits. Since your survival depends on reaching the base, you must decide which existing items will offer the most help. Choose well. Your life depends on it.

Step B

Examine the list of 15 items that survived the forced landing. Rank them in order of importance, with number 1 being the most important item and number 15 the least.

Step C

Now form small groups, discuss the items and rank the list again, by consensus.

Step D

Check the list you did alone and your group list against the NASA ranking your teacher will give you.

Step E

Next, calculate the error in your rankings. Calculate error points as the absolute difference between the NASA (EXPERT) ranking and the individual or group ranking numbers. Total the error in both categories to rate your survival decisions.

Scoring			
0–26	Excellent	46–55	Fair
26–32	Good	56–70	Poor
33–45	Average	71–112	Very Poor

To make educated choices, research the moon at Views of the Solar System.

Moon

URL: http://bang.lanl.gov/solarsys/moon.htm

Items	Your Ranking	Group Ranking	NASA ranking	Your Error	Group Error
Box of matches					
Food concentrate					
50-ft nylon rope					
Parachute					
Portable heating unit					
.45 caliber pistol					
Case of dehydrated milk					
(2) 100 lb tanks of oxygen					
Moon constellation map					
Self-inflating life raft					
Magnetic compass					
5 gal. of water					
Self-igniting signal with flares					
First-Aid Kit with hypodermic needles					
Solar-powered FM transceiver					

Activity Sheet   Surviving a Lunar Crash

Answer Key

NASA Expert Ranking

ITEM	EXPERT RANKING	REASON
Matches	15	No air on moon so matches will not burn
Food concentrate	4	Efficient means of supplying energy requirements
50 ft. nylon robe	6	Useful in scaling cliffs or in case of injury
Parachute	8	Possible use as sun shield
Portable heater	13	Not needed unless on dark side
.45 caliber pistol	11	Possible means of self propulsion
Dehydrated milk	12	Bulkier duplication of energy source
2 100 lb oxygen tanks	1	Most pressing survival requirement
Moon constellation	3	Primary means of navigation map
Self-inflating life raft	9	CO_2 bottle in raft might be used as a propulsion source
Magnetic compass	14	Magnetic fields of moon are not polarized so compass is useless.
5 gal. of water	2	Replacement of tremendous liquid loss on lighted side of moon
Self-igniting signal	10	Distress signal when mother ship flares is sighted
First-aid kit with	7	Needles for medicines and hypodermic needle vitamins fit special suit aperture
Solar-powered FM	5	For communication with mother transceiver ship on line of sight

A Tale about Cockroaches

Student name: _____

Step	A

Go to these sites to find ten scary facts about cockroaches.

A Day in the Life of Rodney Roach
URL: http://www.nj.com/yucky/life/index.html

51 Roach Facts
URL: http://www.nj.com/yucky/facts/index.html

Step	B

List your ten scary facts here:

1. _____

2. _____

3. _____

4. _____

5. _____

6. _____

7. _____

8. _____

9. _____

10. _____

Step	C

Use your ten scary facts to write an original story about cockroaches that includes these facts. But first, read through some of the stories that other students have written about cockroaches to get some more ideas.

Tall Tales

URL: http://www.nj.com/yucky/ttales/index.cgi

Step	D

Begin your story with one of these first sentences, or create your own:

1. I couldn't believe what I saw in my bed when I turned on the light!

2. I woke up in the middle of the night and heard the strangest sound.

3. My life as a cockroach was just about to change in a big way.

4. They were everywhere: scratching and creeping and crawling.

5. As I crawled up the wall on my nightly journey through the kitchen, I spotted a nice, cold piece of pizza in an open box on the kitchen table.

Walk the Dinosaur Through Time

Student name:_____

| **Step** | **A** | In this activity you will change a dinosaur into an animal of your choice, as if it were changing over time. Go to *ION Science News* for |

the *Dinosaurs Live On* article. Use the information presented in the article for this Activity sheet. Choose one of the dinosaurs from below to work with.

ION Science News

URL: http://njw.injersey.com/media/IonSci/index.html

Dinosaurs Live On

URL: http://njw.injersey.com/media/IonSci/features/dino/dino.html

| **Step** | **B** | Choose any animal that you want your dinosaur to have changed into. Draw four pictures of this change through time. Your goal is to |

gradually change from one animal to the other.

| **Step** | **C** | As you draw, features of the dinosaur will slowly fade as features of your chosen animal slowly appear. It does not matter what animal |

you picked as long as you show the change through time.

Social Studies

Lesson Plans,

Activity Sheets,

and Student Handouts

A Note on the Organization

Lesson plans are arranged in alphabetical order, with grade levels indicated in the top left corner.

Student handouts are included with some of the lesson plans and are identified with a computer icon on the top left-hand corner.

Stand-alone activity sheets appear at the end of the chapter.

Archaeological Time Capsule

 ## Overview

In this lesson, your students examine the remains of ancient cultures and predict the future based on their study.

 ## Materials

- None

 ## Objectives

- Research artifacts from ancient Egypt
- Hypothesize why these items have withstood time
- Predict what artifacts future historians will discover from present-day society
- Analyze the environmental and societal factors that contribute to an artifact's survival

Procedures

1 Ask your students if they have ever read a science fiction novel or have ever seen a science-fiction movie depicting a character in the distant future who has discovered artifacts from the 20th century. Ray Bradbury novels or *Planet of the Apes* movies offer a starting point for such a discussion. Often in such science fiction scenarios, the people of the future don't know the original use of the objects they have found.

This is the situation scientists, architects, and archaeologists face today when they debate the design, purpose, origin, and structure of ancient artifacts and structures, such as the monoliths at Stonehenge and Easter Island or the pyramids in Egypt and Central America. So much changes over time that people in the present are often puzzled by the artifacts of the past. Perhaps the archaeologists of the future will have a difficult time determining the function of a coffee can lid or a piece of a space probe.

Brainstorm some of the dramatic changes that occur over time that could cause confusion. In addition to the passage of time, ask your students to consider the history lost when disasters such as fires, earthquakes, invading armies, and epidemics sweep through a culture.

❷ Have your students get into small groups, and send each group to the sites below to gather background on the artifacts of ancient Egypt. Tell them to look at the photos of the pyramids and the sphinxes. Judging from the photos, do these structures appear to be relatively intact? Make sure your students also see the smaller artifacts, such as Tutankhamen's death mask and the burial jewelry the Egyptians created for the afterlife. The ancient Egyptians were masters in preservation. Ask your students to compile a list of artifacts. Then ask them to suggest what purpose each object served the ancient Egyptians. If the purpose is unclear, remind your students that sometimes even the experts are baffled. Tell your students to hypothesize the missing information.

Exhibit of Artifacts
URL: http://www.memphis.edu/egypt/artifact.html

Map of Egypt
URL: http://www.memphis.edu/egypt/map.htm

Ancient Egypt Pictures Hall
URL: http://www.mordor.com/hany/egypt/eg_pics1.html

❸ Now that your students have explored the past, ask them to imagine the artifacts we will leave behind for future civilizations. Consider all our material goods as well as our buildings, roadways, airports, and space centers. What do your students think will survive as a legacy or remnant? Consider also the durability of some items and the changes that can occur over time. Remember, your students have been studying change over time and the effects of change. Any speculation they devise is a hypothesis at best, but they must support their hypotheses with facts from what they learned about the past.

⚙ Extensions

❶ Explore the ancient Mayan civilization at the *Rabbit in the Moon* site for remnants that have stood the test of time as well. Repeat the steps of this lesson, but consider the topographical, societal, and climactic conditions of this area when formulating your thesis.

Rabbit in the Moon
URL: http://www.he.net/~nmcnelly/

❷ Have each of your students create a personal time capsule. Ask them to bring in one cardboard box (2' x 2') with ten items they would like to leave behind so that people of the future will understand more about individuals in the late twentieth century. Ask your students to consider the objects for their time capsule very carefully. For example, if your students would like to choose an audio CD or a cassette tape, they must also leave behind the necessary appliance to play the CD or tape! But what if the civilizations of the future do not have electricity? Will they have technology to convert our technology into their own?

❸ Imagine that pyramids and obelisks once stood near your school. Would these structures have survived the centuries as they have in Egypt and Central America? What environmental and cultural factors could lead to the demise of such structures in other areas of the world? Test your students' reasoning skills!

Archaeological
Time Capsule

- Visit each of the sites below to gather some background on the artifacts of ancient Egypt.

  Exhibit of Artifacts
  URL: http://www.memphis.edu/egypt/artifact.html

  Map of Egypt
  URL: http://www.memphis.edu/egypt/map.htm

  Tour Eqypt
  URL: http://touregypt.net/index.htm

- Look at the photos of the pyramids and the sphinxes. Do these structures seem to be relatively intact? Also look at the smaller artifacts, such as Tutankhamen's death mask and the burial jewelry created for the afterlife.

- Now compile a list of artifacts and what purpose you think these objects served the ancient Egyptians. If the purpose is unclear, don't fret! Experts are still baffled. Hypothesize the missing information.

List of Artifacts	*Egyptians Used Them For*

Balancing the Budget

Overview

Students learn the process of drawing up a balanced budget — for the household and for the United States.

Materials

- Printer
- An economics or government text with budget terms and definitions
- Local and national newspapers (optional, but helpful)

Objectives

- Brainstorm the elements of budget for a household
- Compare the positives/negatives of each spending category
- Work effectively in teams
- Create a budget proposal
- Rationalize budget choices

Procedures

1 Begin your lesson with the discussion prompt: "What if you could control how every single dollar in your household is spent?" Let your students decide on the budget categories themselves. Flesh out a list of spending categories and their relevant importance in the total spending picture; when all categories have been decided on by your students, ask them to consider some items they may have missed. Make a circle or line graph on the board to illustrate your class's budget. At this point, do not worry about financial figures; just record the categories and percentage allotments for total spending. This gives your class a good picture of how budget is determined and maintained, on any level from personal to global.

2 Tell your students that they will propose their own simulated budget on a national level using national spending categories. Log on to the *CCER National Budget Simulation* WWW site and read the instructions. Choose one of the two sites to run your budget simulation. The monetary figures are not provided until after you propose your budget, so your students will not know how much of the total expenditures each category entails at first.

CCER National Budget Simulation
URL: http://garnet.berkeley.edu:3333/budget/budget.html

3 Have your students break into teams and play the short version of the simulation; make sure they read the hypertext descriptions of the spending categories so they know where their money is going! They should keep notes on how they changed the spending on each category and why: why did they feel that they should reduce military spending while increasing the space technology spending, etc.? Make sure your students supply their rationale for making the changes they do. Have your students submit their proposals and view the actual financial figures and changes. Have your student groups log their new figures on the board and explain what they cut and added. Let your class vote on the feasibility of each group's budget choices; choose the most practical one and compare and contrast it to President Clinton's actual budget proposal for 1998.

FY97 Budget
URL: http://www.doc.gov/BudgetFY97/bud97toc.html

⬛ Extensions

➊ For more information, background, and insight on the Federal Budget, check out these Internet sites!

A Citizen's Guide to the Federal Budget
URL: gopher://sunny.statusa.gov:70/00/BudgetFY96/bud96g.txt

Budget FY96 (budget information for 1996 fiscal year)
URL: gopher://gopher.esa.doc.gov/11/BudgetFY96

➋ Obtain a copy of SimCity (or any of the Sim series simulations by Maxis) for more in-depth practice of budget, city planning *et al.* You can find information, including teaching tips, at the *Maxis* WWW site!

Maxis Home Page
URL: http://www.maxis.com/index.html

➌ Run the long version of the budget simulator after researching the finer details of budget from the above sites; there is much more accurate spending brackets, therefore there are much more ramifications of each budget choice!

National Budget Simulation: Long Version
URL: http://garnet.berkeley.edu:6997/longbudget.html

Learning Japanese

Overview

Students explore the Japanese culture and language.

Materials

- Printer
- Flash cards
- Poster board

Objectives

- Contribute "slang" words
- Foster multicultural awareness
- Pronounce Japanese words for common animals and food

Procedures

1 Begin a discussion with your class centered on "slang" words and symbols: secret words that your students may use when speaking with each other. For example, if a student says, "My T.V. rules!", he or she may be saying that their television is of an excellent quality, not that the appliance imposes supreme sovereign dominance of any sort. These words and their uses may be "foreign" to you as an adult, but to your students they are commonplace, colorful ways to communicate. Write some of the words on the board with their definition or a symbol for easy recognition. This is "another" language that your students have "mastered!"

❷ Tell your students that they will learn a new alphabet today: Hiragana, the simplest Japanese character language. Log on to the *Kid's Window* WWW site and surf to the *Kid's Window School/Language Class/Hiragana* page. Here you'll find the symbols, pronunciations, sample words, and guides for writing each symbol. Have your students write each symbol in freehand, play the sound file for pronunciation, and listen to some Japanese words that use that character. An easy way to categorize the sounds is by vowel sound, from left to right on the chart: *a, i, u, e, o*. From top left to bottom left, the characters are arranged by consonant sound.

Kid's Window
URL: http://jw.stanford.edu/KIDS/kids_home.html

Let's Learn Hiragana
URL: http://jw.stanford.edu/KIDS/SCHOOL/LANG/hira/

❸ When your students have practiced each character and sound, have them create flash cards with the symbols and pronunciations, then practice the Hiragana as a group recitation — the same way children learn the ABCs! Make this a daily part of your activities. Young children have the propensity to learn and retain foreign languages; your classroom can be the genesis for building and maintaining lifelong multicultural awareness.

☒ Extensions

❶ Surf the rest of the *Kid's Window* site and learn how to pronounce names for animals, what Japanese meals consist of, and read an interactive Japanese children's story. Maintain your class recitation skills throughout as these sections of *Kid's Window* include the Japanese words as well as English.

❷ Go to the grocery store with your class to find ingredients for a Japanese breakfast as described on the site; cook and enjoy it with your class one morning! Make sure your class and you use the proper "eating" words in Japanese while you enjoy your meal.

❸ Let your class practice their new-found language skills over the Internet via email or CuSeeMe with a QuickCam and CuSeeMe software. Your class can communicate with Japanese citizens and students, who in turn can teach your class more of the language and culture in exchange for your students' aid to them with the English language and culture. Set up your session with the following groups.

The Japanese Education Usenet newsgroup
URL: news:fj.education

Cornell University's CU-SeeMe Page
URL: http://cu-seeme.cornell.edu/Welcome.html

❹ For more information on Japanese language and culture, check out these WWW sites!

Japanese Information
URL: http://www.ntt.jp/japan/index.html

Traveler's Japanese with Voice
URL: http://www.ntt.jp/japan/japanese/

Seven Wonders

Past and Present

Overview

This lesson uses the seven wonders of the ancient world as a springboard for cultural exploration as students select and present their own seven wonders in modern life.

Materials

- Poster board
- Drawing or painting materials
- Optional: video camera, HyperCard Stack software, camera, tape recorder

Objectives

- Identify the seven wonders of the ancient world
- Justify the choices of these wonders
- Select the greatest wonder of the ancient world
- Work effectively in groups
- Create a list of seven new wonders in the present time and in everyday life
- Present and explain these new modern wonders of the world

Procedures

1 Ask your students to think for a few moments about the greatest buildings, places, or things they've seen. They can choose their wonders from anything they have seen firsthand on field trips, summer vacations, visits to museums, parks, cities, mountains, beaches, etc. Explain that for centuries people have identified the man-made or natural objects they consider amazing. Tell your students that today they will study what has become known as the "Seven Wonders of the Ancient World." Also tell them they will go on to select their own wonders of the modern world.

❷ Group your students into pairs and have each group go to this site.

The Seven Wonders of the Ancient World
URL: http://pharos.bu.edu/Egypt/Wonders/

Ask each group to view all seven wonders, and briefly explain why they think the ancients selected them as wonders. Ask your students to consider the location, structure, beauty, magnitude, and duration of each wonder when they are writing. One detailed paragraph for each wonder will be sufficient. Make sure your students see the beautiful graphics accompanying each one.

After all your students have written their paragraphs on the seven wonders of the ancient world, ask them to share their ideas in an open discussion. Try to determine what your class considers the greatest of the ancient wonders by taking a vote. Remember, your students are free to disagree! This could turn into a lively, interactive debate.

❸ Now that your students have evaluated the wonders of the ancients, challenge the student pairs to create a list of the seven wonders in their own lives and experiences. This will return the lesson to your original discussion prompt. Tell your students to only select wonders they have seen firsthand. After they make their choices, they will need to research the facts about their selection in the library. Tell your students that each student pair will be explaining their choices in a class presentation. If your class has the time and technology, your students can deliver elaborate, detailed reports using sounds, pictures, videos, or Hypercard Stack presentations; or your students can deliver an oral presentation with a poster they've drawn showing the wonders. Since your students have different tastes and have visited different places and seen different things, you should find some variety in their selection of wonders.

⬢ Extensions

1 Have your students imagine they have unlimited money and an inexhaustible labor force to construct their own wonder for people today and in the future to view. Would your student erect ninety-foot statues of themselves on roller blades, or would they create the world's most perfect city? Let their imaginations go wild.

2 Have your students go to this Web site to find the location of each of the seven wonders.

Location of the Seven Wonders
URL: http://pharos.bu.edu/Egypt/Wonders/map.html

Your students can do further research on the geography of this area and in your school library. Ask your students to consider why all the wonders are located in one general area. Your students can research the climate, topography, and culture to generate their own theories about why the wonders of the ancient world are located in the Mediterranean region.

Some great starting points on the Internet:

Ancient City of Athens
URL: http://www.indiana.edu/~kglowack/Athens/Athens.html

The Egyptian Gallery
URL: http://www.mordor.com/hany/egypt/egypt.html

The Institute of Egyptian Art and Archaeology
URL: http://www.memphis.edu/egypt/main.html

Another great ancient world site with similarities to the ancient Mediterranean world to explore:

Rabbit in the Moon: Mayan Glyphs and Architecture
URL: http://www.he.net/~nmcnelly/

3 Turn this lesson into a school-wide project to name the seven wonders of your town or area. Ask the entire student body to nominate their choices for the seven wonders. From that list, create a ballot, and have each student vote for their seven favorites. From that vote, you can determine the seven wonders of your area. Have the students create an exhibit for the school or for the community.

Seven Wonders

Past and Present

- With a partner, go to this Web site:

  The Seven Wonders of the Ancient World
  URL: http://pharos.bu.edu/Egypt/Wonders/

- Look at all seven wonders. After you've seen everything, write a detailed paragraph about each wonder explaining why you think the ancients selected it. Consider the location, structure, beauty, magnitude, and duration of each wonder when you are writing your paragraphs. When you finish, your teacher will ask you to share your ideas with the class.

- After the class discussion is over, you and your partner should create a list of what you consider to be seven wonders in the present time. Only select wonders you or your partner have seen firsthand. You will probably need to research your wonders in your school or community library, or ask local historians.

- When you finish your research, you and your partner will present your own seven wonders, with explanation and visual aides, to the class. Depending on the time you have to work on this project, you can deliver an elaborate, detailed description using pictures, sounds, videos, or Hypercard Stack presentations.

<table>
<tr><td>LESSON PLAN
Grades 5–9</td><td></td></tr>
</table>

Symbolism in Architecture

Overview

This lesson allows your students to explore the concept of symbolism in architecture as they discover functional and symbolic meanings for five ancient structures.

Materials

- Computer with Internet access
- Color printer

Objectives

- Gather data on five ancient architectural structures
- Hypothesize about what each structure symbolized to the culture that erected it
- Realize how ancient cultures inspire and influence the present

Procedures

1 Show your students a picture of the Capitol building in Washington, D.C. Ask your students to offer their knowledge of this famous building. Explain that this famous building was built in the classical architectural style. Ask your students why this building and other important buildings are often built in this classic style. Discuss the Capitol building as a symbol of the United States of America and of democracy, strength, and unity. Ask your students how the architect styled the building to show these features. Ask your students what else the building might symbolize. Many public buildings, from courthouses to banks to universities, have been built in a similar classical style. Discuss a few buildings in your city and what their architectural style might symbolize. After this activity, your students will understand and be able to define the concept of symbolism.

❷ Have each of your students go to these sites to select five ancient buildings. Tell them to gather information on all five. Your students can find the information at the sites and in your school library or media center. Next have your students write a paragraph about each. (If you wish, they can also print out the graphics of the five sites they have selected.) In the paragraph, your students should include facts about each building, their thoughts about what its style symbolized to the ancient culture, and whether its style continues to be an influence on architecture today.

Institute of Egyptian Art and Architecture
URL: http://www.memphis.edu/egypt/main.html

Ancient City of Athens
URL: http://www.indiana.edu/~kglowack/Athens/Athens.html

Tour Egypt
URL: http://touregypt.net/index.htm

The Seven Wonders of the Ancient World
URL: http://pharos.bu.edu/Egypt/Wonders/

Rabbit in the Moon: Mayan Glyphs and Architecture
URL: http://www.he.net/~nmcnelly/

❸ After your students complete their five paragraphs, have each student briefly share their findings with the class. Ask your class to discuss the original ideals these buildings represented. Has the original symbolism of the buildings survived? What has been lost? Do these structures influence architects today? Ask your students if they are surprised that structures so ancient continue to provide inspiration today. After hearing about all these ancient buildings, your class will realize ancient cultures continue to influence us today.

◘ Extensions

❶ Have your students list five buildings in your area or five buildings they have seen while traveling. Then ask them to write an essay about the five structures including a physical description and a symbolic interpretation of each building. For example, post offices often have a certain look that distinguishes them from other buildings. Where and when did the style originate? How does its appearance impress and influence those who use the building?

❷ Symbolism is usually a concept taught in Language Arts class. Discuss the concept of symbolism with your class as it pertains to the art, music, and writings from these ancient cultures. Why not create a team-teaching opportunity with your Language Arts, Math, and Art teachers for a week-long integrated unit on symbols in society?

❸ Have your students surf this site to find artifacts. For a great exercise using high-level thinking and imagination, allow your students to hypothesize the symbolism as well as the function of the artifacts they have found. Tell them they can find symbols manifested in physical forms in all cultures and society throughout history, even at this site. To check for understanding, give your students ten items and tell them to define their physical and symbolic meanings. This would make a great test idea.

Exhibit of Artifacts
URL: http://www.memphis.edu/egypt/artifact.html

❹ The mythologies of the ancient cultures offer another view into the lives, practices, and beliefs of cultures far removed from our own. Have your students go to your media center or library to research the mythologies of the ancient Greeks, Egyptians, and Mayans. Your students can begin their search at these sites.

Rabbit in the Moon
URL: http://www.he.net/~nmcnelly/moon.html

Symbolism in Architecture

- Go to these Web sites and select five ancient buildings you like.

Institute of Egyptian Art and Architecture
URL: http://www.memphis.edu/egypt/main.html

Ancient City of Athens
URL: http://www.indiana.edu/~kglowack/Athens/Athens.html

The Egyptian Gallery
URL: http://www.mordor.com/hany/egypt/egypt.html

The Seven Wonders of the Ancient World
URL: http://pharos.bu.edu/Egypt/Wonders/

Rabbit in the Moon: Mayan Glyphs and Architecture
URL: http://www.he.net/~nmcnelly/

- Gather information on each of the buildings you've chosen. You can find information on the Web sites and in your school library.

- Now write a paragraph about each of your buildings. In each paragraph, include your facts about the building, your thoughts about what its style might have symbolized to the ancients, and whether its style influences architecture today. Share what you've written with your class.

Titanic
Unsinkable?

Overview

This unit features a variety of higher level thinking activities based on the tragic sinking of the *Titanic* oceanliner.

Materials

- Printer

Objectives

- Analyze the structure and provisions of the great ship
- Create and/or justify theories on the sinking of the *Titanic*
- Hypothesize how the ship and its passengers could have been saved
- Utilize problem-solving skills to build an "unsinkable" *Titanic*

Procedures

1 Start an open discussion with your students with the prompt: "How do we know we are safe?" All humans take risks every day: driving to work, playing football, taking prescription drugs, etc. Who determines the "safety" inherent in any activity? Lead your class to the issue that the designers, builders, crew, and passengers all thought that the *Titanic* was unsinkable. The ship, as fate would prove, was not unsinkable. Ask your students to mull this point over for five minutes in a free-writing session. Ask them to consider the actions they take in life every day that are said to be safe, and how that security affects them. Sometimes, merely a confident advertising is all that is necessary to instill lack of fear in a product. "Four out of five dentists recommend…"

❷ Have your students group into small research and proposal teams and log on to *The Titanic Home Page* on the WWW to research the dimensions and logistics of the ship, theories why she sank, and consider the veracity of the theories while they surf the site. Was the ship just too large and unruly? Were there accurate provisions? Was the crew acting responsibly, or were they merely behaving in accordance to the supreme confidence of the ship's "unsinkability?" Where there enough lifeboats to support the entire group of passengers? Was the captain negligent? Could a more feasible course have been charted? Let your students amass these and other questions and formulate their own theory, whether or not they agree with the theories presented. For more information, research some of the other *Titanic* sites. Download and print the text and graphics for support.

The *Titanic* Home Page
URL: http://gil.ipswichcity.qld.gov.au/~dalgarry/

Virtual *Titanic*
URL: http://www.discovery.com/DCO/doc/1012/world/specials/
    titanic/titanic1.7.html

In Memoriam: R.M.S. Titanic
URL: http://www.xnet.com/~cmd/titanic/

❸ Allow your students to utilize their theories and create a more "unsinkable" *Titanic*. They can use existing technology if they wish. Let them be creative and imaginative in their proposals, as long as they support their theories with facts from the sites. Compile and amalgamate the proposals into one class ship: a "New Titanic."

Extensions

1 You can have your "New Titanic" built for you by a professional online model company. Email them your exact specifications and they will build a high-quality model and ship it to your school for displaying in your classroom!

Stuart Miles, ABL Ship Models
URL: mailto:stuart@transend.com.tw

2 Research the other ships of the White Star line on *The Titanic Home Page*. Determine if they, too shared the same unfortunate fate as did the *Titanic*. Was this line a success? What are some of the traits shared by these ships?

3 Email your theories on the sinking of the *Titanic* and your proposals that may have made the *Titanic* a success story rather than a disaster. Your students' theories will be published on the WWW site!
URL: mailto:dalgarry@gil.ipswichcity.qld.gov.au

4 Coordinate your lesson with your students' math teacher; determine how much provision would be needed for a ship with twice the passengers as the *Titanic,* with one-third the amount, etc. How much provision would have been necessary for a three month voyage? You can find this data on *The Titanic Home Page* site.

5 Have your students imagine they were a passenger on the sinking ship; ask them to compose letters home from three different viewpoints: on the night before the ship sank, from inside the lifeboat (if they were one of the lucky ones...), and several days later from the hospital. Urge them to write vividly and imaginatively; try to capture the unfounded confidence and merriment before, the sheer terror during, and the reflection after the tragic accident.

Virtual Family Tree

Overview

Students research their family history and assume the role of a genealogist online.

Materials

- Computer with Internet access
- Large posterboard
- Markers
- Student-provided photographs or copies of photographs

Objectives

- Gather and research family data
- Create a family tree with photographs and statistics
- Research and assume the role of a genealogist online
- Search for possible distant family members on the Internet
- Optional: contact possible family members via email or snail mail

Procedures

1 Have your students make a "rough draft" family tree that includes their immediate family, uncles, aunts, cousins, and grandparents. The more information your students can gather about their family, the better. Encourage them to gather information on where their family members were born, where they lived, and where they died, if applicable. Make sure your students carefully gather all their family members' surnames and maiden names. Ask your students to paste or tape photographs of their family members on the white posterboard and draw a map of their immediate family. Give your students several days to complete this tree, then continue this lesson.

❷ When your students have completed their family trees, tell them that they will be acting the role of a professional online genealogist! Ask your students to exchange their family trees and do some background reading at these sites so they can effectively "find" lost or unknown family members of their "clients": their fellow classmates. Your students should read through these pages and take the appropriate notes they'll need for their search. Your students can learn valuable tips that real genealogists use, both on the Internet and in real life.

The Genealogy Resource Page
URL: http://html.tamu.edu:8000/~mbg5500/genealogy/
    lds_gen_info.html

Genealogy Page
URL: http://www.sunset.net/meyerj/me01003.html

Genealogy: Everton Publishing
URL: http://www.everton.com

❸ Now that your students have immersed themselves in the world of genealogical searching, have them do an electronic information search on the Internet. There are incredible search pages on the World Wide Web just waiting to be explored! Your students should search these databases with the surnames of the family members and information on where they live (or lived) to find possible relatives. Your students will be amazed at how many people in the world have the very same names as they do! Of course, these are only the listings of people online, or data published online from commercial vendors; a scrutinously detailed genealogical search would entail much legwork through old cemeteries and dusty town hall registries, but this online search is a great start that they can accomplish from the (relative) comfort of their desk.

WhoWhere Email Addresses
URL: http://www.whowhere.com/

Four 11 Directory Services
URL: http://www.Four11.com/

People Search
URL: http://pages.ripco.com:8080/~glr/stalk.html

4 Have each student fill in the names and locations of potential family members they've found in their search and return the completed "family tree" back to the client for whom they've done the search.

Extensions

1 Have your students email or snail mail some or all of these possible family members. Your students should introduce themselves and members of their family that live in that area to see if they are related. Set up an acceptable, nonoffensive questionnaire with your students to ensure their safety, as well as ensuring that the people that are being emailed are not "put out." Encourage your students to be courteous and thank everyone in advance for their time. You could even have your students send a "virtual bouquet" as a greeting to their potential family members from this site!

Virtual Bouquet
URL: http://www.virtualflowers.com

2 Your students can study some of the largest "family relocation" events in history on the World Wide Web and in your school's media center: the diaspora for Jewish people, immigration at Ellis Island, slave trade for Africans, and the potato famines for the Irish, for example. Have your students do a keyword search for the topic pertaining to their family's history; help your students narrow and restrict their searches!

Alta Vista Search Engine
URL: http://www.altavista.digital.com/

3 For more information on genealogy, have your students get some tips and share techniques with people engrossed in searching for their family by checking into this Usenet Newsgroup.

Usenet Genealogy Newsgroup
URL: news:alt.genealogy

War Letters

Overview

Students compare and contrast letters from soldiers in two wars: the Civil War and the Vietnam War. Activities include writing fictitious war letters and formulating a thesis on the nature of war.

Materials

• Printer

Objectives

• Identify and utilize the components of a letter
• Identify point of view, voice, tone, and style in letter writing
• Compare and contrast letters from the Civil War and Vietnam War
• Formulate a thesis on the unchanging nature of war as viewed through the eyes of a soldier

Procedures

❶ Ask your students if they've ever been away from home for an extended period of time: summer camp, travel abroad, a weekend when their parents were away on a trip, etc.; let them relay their feelings of "homesickness" and fear of the unknown, as well as their excitement of being in a new place and a new situation. Keep track of some of the positive and negative emotions your students have felt in these situations. Ask your students to figure in the threat of losing their life at any moment along with those feelings. This is the beginning of understanding how a soldier, constantly in fear for his life, feels in battle.

2 Pair your students off at your computers and connect to the *Letters Home from a Soldier in the U.S. Civil War* site and read some of the letters home, especially the earliest and latest. Ask your student pairs to notate how they felt the tone is conveyed, and how the style reads. Nineteenth century writers used a voice a bit different than our present writing voice. Your students should briefly summarize the letter: its intent and message. Ask your students to identify the components of a letter format.

Letters Home from a Soldier in the U.S. Civil War
URL: http://www.ucsc.edu/civil-war-letters/home.html

3 Repeat the procedure, this time for a letter home from Vietnam from a soldier to his mother: *There Really is a War*. Ask your students to consider the same elements of writing, identify the intent and message, and this time compare and contrast the two voices. Are the two soldiers' situations, hopes, and fears much different over the course of one hundred years? What are the similarities and/or differences? Your students can use the data they've collected in pairs to formulate a thesis and support that would address this issue. One hundred years of technology and changing times is not so long....

There Really is a War
URL: http://grunt.space.swri.edu:80/tbomlet.htm

🖧 Extensions

1 Each student can choose one of the soldiers' point of view and compose an imaginative letter to the other, as if they could communicate with each other, reflecting on that soldier's time period, but also adding some suggestions and tips on how to survive the ordeal. Collect these letters and post them around the room; see if any of the trends reflect the real soldiers' letters.

2 View the film *Glory* or *Gettysburg* and read excerpts from *Letters From Home* for more in-depth, graphic descriptions of these two conflicts. For more information, check out some of these related sites.

Letters of William H. Jackson
URL: http://www.access.digex.net/~bdboyle/wjackson.html

Civil War Letters of J.C. Cohen
URL: http://www.access.digex.net/~bdboyle/cohen.html

Top's Tent (Vietnam experiences)
URL: http://grunt.space.swri.edu:80/ttintro.htm

Images of My War (Vietnam experiences)
URL: http://grunt.space.swri.edu:80/vnbktoc.htm

3 Compose a letter or interview to post on the Veterans Usenet newsgroup; here, your students can speak with real veterans from WWI to the Persian Gulf War. Your class could research the similarities and differences among these soldiers' stories and tap into a "living textbook" of information.

Veterans Usenet Newsgroup
URL: news:soc.veterans

Activity
Sheet
Grades
5–8

Pictures from the Past

Student name:_____

Step	A

Use your super-sleuthing searching abilities to find the answers to the ten questions listed below. Go to the *Ancient Egypt Pictures Hall* Web page to find the answers. Good luck!

Ancient Egypt Pictures Hall
URL: http://www.interactive.net/~hany/egypt/eg_pics1.html

1. Who is the Egyptian god of the dead? Describe his appearance.

_____

_____

_____

2. How is the palette of King Narmer typical of how ancient Egyptian artists glorified the pharaoh in their work?

_____

_____

_____

3. What was the name of the hardest stone available at the time of the Old Kingdom in Egypt?

_____

4. Who was the pharaoh of Egypt from 1279 to 1212 B.C.? Why is he remembered?

_____

_____

5. What does the illustration of the wall painting from Thebes tell you how the nobility were treated? Compare this to what you know about the treatment of the gentry in the rural South before the Civil War.

_____

_____

_____

_____

6. Why do you think Tutankhamen's mask is so elaborate? What does this tell you about the ancient Egyptian view of death? Does the modern world emulate this view today?

_____

_____

_____

_____

7. Who ruled during Egypt's 12th dynasty from 1842 to 1797 B.C.? How is his sculpture "realistic" compared to the sculptures of other Egyptian pharaohs of different times?

_____

_____

_____

_____

8. When were the pyramids constructed? What was so special about the ancient Egyptian engineers who built them?

_____

_____

_____

_____

9. What is the oldest royal tomb in Egypt and one of the oldest stone structures in Egypt? How does it differ from the other royal tombs on this site?

_____

_____

_____

_____

_____

10. During the Amarna period, sculpted figures were not "idealized." The artists did not attempt to glorify the pharaohs by making them appear more beautiful or strong. How does the statue of Akhenaton and Nefertiti illustrate this?

_____

_____

_____

_____

_____

_____

Athens Travel Brochure

Student name: _____

| Step | A |

The city of Athens has hired you to write a travel brochure to boost tourism. You'll be selecting one of the areas in the topography and monuments segment of the *Ancient City of Athens* site as the subject for your travel brochure. Each section of this site has photographs and text describing the area, but the topography and monuments segment takes an academic approach to ancient Athens. Surf through it to find the area you'd like as the subject of your travel brochure. In your brochure, you're going to make your part of Athens seem like the hippest place in the world. You want to lure more tourists to Athens.

Ancient City of Athens

URL: http://www.indiana.edu/~kglowack/Athens/Athens.html

| Step | B |

After you've selected the area of Athens for your travel brochure, think of how you can describe it to attract tourism. Think about all the special interests and needs that would need to be included in a successful travel brochure. You'll have to use your imagination to fill in the details along with the facts you learn about Athens on the site and in your library.

Here's an outline to get you started:

(Name of area)

1. Accommodations from hotels to campgrounds. Tell your readers where they might stay and what it will cost.

_____

_____

_____

2. Attractions from museums to theaters. Your readers want to know what they shouldn't miss, what these attractions cost, and when these places are open.

_____

_____

_____

3. Food from fancy restaurants to food stalls on the streets. Your readers need suggestions about where to eat and how much to expect to pay.

_____

_____

_____

4. Outdoor recreation from parks to beaches. Your readers want to know if they can hit the beach after a day in a museum.

_____

_____

_____

5. Shopping. Your readers need to know where they can buy cool stuff to bring home.

_____

_____

_____

6. Maps. Your readers need to know how to find the attractions you suggest and how they can get to them by bus, subway, or bike.

_____

_____

_____

Activity Sheet   Athens Travel Brochure

7. Local transportation. Your readers need to know if they can get to the attractions you suggest by bus, subway, taxi, or by foot.

_____

_____

_____

8. Entertainment. If there's a club known for its great Greek music, tell your readers.

_____

_____

_____

9. Insider's Travel Tips (OK, what are the real "goods" on Athens?)

_____

_____

_____

Step	C

Take the material you've gathered above to create the copy for your travel brochure. Travel brochures need pictures, so collect some of the images on the site, or draw your own illustrations.

Activity Sheet Athens Travel Brochure

Glossary

Acceptable Use Policy (AUP)
A written agreement signed by teachers, students, and parents outlining terms and conditions of Internet use.

Commercial online service
A company that, for a fee, allows computer users to dial in via modem to access its information and services, which now includes indirect access to the Internet. Examples are America Online and Prodigy.

Database
A computer holding large amounts of information that can be searched by an Internet user.

Download/upload
Download: transferring (retrieving) a file from another computer to the your computer. *Upload:* sending a file to another computer.

Emoticons
Smileys and other character art that are used to express feelings in email communication —such as :-)

Frequently Asked Questions (FAQ)
Files at many locations on the Net that answer commonly asked questions on hundreds of Internet-related topics. The ftp site below holds every FAQ on the Net.

URL: ftp://rtfm.mit.edu/pub/usenet/

Gopher
A menu-based system for browsing text information on the Internet. Less used today because of the advent of the World Wide Web

Home page
The first Web page that a user sees when visiting a World Wide Web site. Akin to a table of contents or main menu to a Web site.

Hypertext/hyperlink
A highlighted word or graphic in a Web document that, when clicked upon, takes the user to a related piece of information on the Internet.

Infobot (or mailbot)
An email address that automatically returns information requested by the user. Akin to a real-world fax-back service.

Internet
The global computer network that connects more than four million computers in over 160 countries. The Internet is the virtual "space" in which users can send and receive email, browse databases of information (gopher, World Wide Web), and send and receive programs (ftp) and files.

Internet Service Provider (ISP)
Any organization that provides access to the Internet. ISPs also offer technical assistance to schools that want to become Internet sites and place their information online. A list of ISPs can be searched via the Web.

URL: http://thelist.iworld.com

Internet site
A computer connected to the Internet and containing information that can be accessed using an Internet navigation tool.

Netiquette
The rules of conduct for Internet users.

Universal Resource Locator (URL)
The address and method used to locate a specific resource on the Internet. A URL beginning with http:// indicates that the site is a Web resource and that a Web browser will access it.

Web Browser
(Also known as Internet Browser or Browser) Software that allows computer users to access and navigate the contents of the Internet. Commercial online services like America Online and Prodigy have their own graphical Internet browsers. Users who access the Internet directly primarily use the Netscape Internet browser to get around online.

World Wide Web (WWW or Web)
A revolutionary Internet navigation system that allows for point-and-click "browsing" or "mining" of the Internet. The WWW is a spiderweb-like interconnection of millions of pieces of information located on computers around the world. Web documents use hypertext, which incorporates text and graphical "links" to other documents and files on Internet-connected computers.

Lesson Plans

Organized by Grade Level

Kindergarten

Language Arts
Ladle Rat Rotten Hut: Jabberwocky
    for Kids, *6*
Wormy Poetry, *41*

Science
Worms: Nature's Recyclers, *89*
Walk the Dinosaur through Time, *102*

Social Studies
Learning Japanese, *111*

First Grade

Language Arts
Ladle Rat Rotten Hut: Jabberwocky
    for Kids, *6*
Wormy Poetry, *41*

Science
Worms: Nature's Recyclers, *89*
Walk the Dinosaur through Time, *102*

Social Studies
Learning Japanese, *111*

Second Grade

Language Arts
Ladle Rat Rotten Hut: Jabberwocky
    for Kids, *6*
Wormy Poetry, *41*

Mathematics
It's the Method that Counts, *51*

Science
Worms: Nature's Recyclers, *89*
A Tale about Cockroaches, *100*
Walk the Dinosaur through Time, *102*

Social Studies
Learning Japanese, *111*

Third Grade

Language Arts
Ladle Rat Rotten Hut: Jabberwocky
    for Kids, *6*
Wormy Poetry, *41*

Mathematics
It's the Method that Counts, *51*

Science
Microscope: Find the Pictures, *78*
Worms: Nature's Recyclers, *89*
A Tale about Cockroaches, *100*
Walk the Dinosaur through Time, *102*

Social Studies
Learning Japanese, *111*

Fourth Grade

Language Arts
Ladle Rat Rotten Hut: Jabberwocky
    for Kids, *6*
Wormy Poetry, *41*

Mathematics
It's the Method that Counts, *51*
Let's Paint!, *54*

Science
The Great Sharks: Misunderstood
    and On Trial!, *71*
Microscope: Find the Pictures, *78*
We Love Cockroaches!, *85*
Worms: Nature's Recyclers, *89*
Meteor Puzzle, *93*
Surviving a Lunar Crash, *97*
A Tale about Cockroaches, *100*
Walk the Dinosaur through Time, *102*

Social Studies
Learning Japanese, *111*
Seven Wonders: Past and Present, *114*
Virtual Family Tree, *125*

Fifth Grade

Language Arts
Poetry in Motion, *14*

Mathematics
It's the Method that Counts, *51*
Let's Paint!, *54*

Science
The Great Sharks: Misunderstood
　　and On Trial!, *71*
Microscope: Find the Pictures, *78*
We Love Cockroaches!, *85*
Meteor Puzzle, *93*
Surviving a Lunar Crash, *97*
Walk the Dinosaur through Time, *102*

Social Studies
Seven Wonders: Past and Present, *114*
Symbolism in Architecture, *118*
Virtual Family Tree, *125*
Pictures from the Past, *131*

Sixth Grade

Language Arts
Poetry in Motion, *14*
Sensory Images in Poetry, *28*

Mathematics
It's the Method that Counts, *51*
Let's Paint!, *54*

Science
The Great Sharks: Misunderstood
　　and On Trial!, *71*
Lab Lightning, *74*
Microscope: Find the Pictures, *78*
We Love Cockroaches!, *85*
Meteor Puzzle, *93*
Surviving a Lunar Crash, *97*
Walk the Dinosaur through Time, *102*

Social Studies
Archaeological Time Capsule, *104*
Seven Wonders: Past and Present, *114*
Symbolism in Architecture, *118*
Virtual Family Tree, *125*
Pictures from the Past, *131*

Seventh Grade

Language Arts
Masculine/Feminine Word Choices, *10*
Poetry in Motion, *14*
The Poet's View of Death, *18*
Sensory Images in Poetry, *28*
His and Hers: Two Views of Love, *38*

Mathematics
Geometric Probability, *47*

Science
The Great Sharks: Misunderstood
　　and On Trial!, *71*
Lab Lightning, *74*
Meteor Puzzle, *93*
Surviving a Lunar Crash, *97*

Social Studies
Archaeological Time Capsule, *104*
Seven Wonders: Past and Present, *114*
Symbolism in Architecture, *118*
Virtual Family Tree, *125*
Pictures from the Past, *131*

Eighth Grade

Language Arts
Masculine/Feminine Word Choices, *10*
Poetry in Motion, *14*
The Poet's View of Death, *18*
Romeo and Juliet: A Production
　　Company Simulation, *22*
Sensory Images in Poetry, *28*
His and Hers: Two Views of Love, *38*

Eighth Grade *(cont.)*

Mathematics
Exploring π, *44*
Geometric Probability, *47*
Solving Word Problems, *61*

Science
The Great Sharks: Misunderstood
    and On Trial!, *71*
Lab Lightning, *74*
Tour the Circulatory System, *82*
Meteor Puzzle, *93*
Surviving a Lunar Crash, *97*

Social Studies
Archaeological Time Capsule, *104*
Seven Wonders: Past and Present, *114*
Symbolism in Architecture, *118*
Virtual Family Tree, *125*
Pictures from the Past, *131*
Athens Travel Brochure, *135*

Ninth Grade

Language Arts
Hamlet on Trial: Innocent, Guilty,
    or Insane? *2*
Masculine/Feminine Word Choices, *10*
The Poet's View of Death, *18*
Romeo and Juliet: A Production
    Company Simulation, *22*
Sensory Images in Poetry, *28*
William Shakespeare: Bard or Bogus? *32*
Aging and the Poetry of W.B. Yeats , *36*
His and Hers: Two Views of Love, *38*

Mathematics
Exploring π, *44*

Mathematics
Geometric Probability, *47*
Similar Triangles, *57*
Solving Word Problems, *61*

Science

Acceleration and the Earth's Gravity, *66*
Lab Lightning, *74*
Tour the Circulatory System, *82*
Surviving a Lunar Crash, *97*

Social Studies
Archaeological Time Capsule, *104*
Balancing the Budget, *108*
Symbolism in Architecture, *118*
Titanic: Unsinkable? *122*
Athens Travel Brochure, *135*

Tenth Grade

Language Arts
Hamlet on Trial: Innocent, Guilty,
    or Insane? *2*
Masculine/Feminine Word Choices, *10*
The Poet's View of Death, *18*
Romeo and Juliet: A Production
    Company Simulation, *22*
Sensory Images in Poetry, *28*
William Shakespeare: Bard or Bogus? *32*
Aging and the Poetry of W.B. Yeats , *36*
His and Hers: Two Views of Love, *38*

Mathematics
Exploring π, *44*
Similar Triangles, *57*
Solving Word Problems, *61*

Science
Acceleration and the Earth's Gravity, *66*
Tour the Circulatory System, *82*
Surviving a Lunar Crash, *97*

Social Studies
Archaeological Time Capsule, *104*
Balancing the Budget, *108*
Titanic: Unsinkable? *122*
War Letters, *128*
Athens Travel Brochure, *135*

Eleventh Grade

Language Arts
Hamlet on Trial: Innocent, Guilty,
    or Insane? *2*
Masculine/Feminine Word Choices, *10*
Sensory Images in Poetry, *28*
William Shakespeare: Bard or Bogus? *32*
Aging and the Poetry of W.B. Yeats , *36*

Mathematics
Exploring π, *44*
Similar Triangles, *57*
Solving Word Problems, *61*

Science
Acceleration and the Earth's Gravity, *66*
Tour the Circulatory System, *82*
Surviving a Lunar Crash, *97*

Social Studies
Balancing the Budget, *108*
Titanic: Unsinkable? *122*
War Letters, *128*
Athens Travel Brochure, *135*

Twelfth Grade

Language Arts
Hamlet on Trial: Innocent, Guilty,
    or Insane? *2*
Masculine/Feminine Word Choices, *10*
Sensory Images in Poetry, *28*
William Shakespeare: Bard or Bogus? *32*
Aging and the Poetry of W.B. Yeats, *36*

Mathematics
Similar Triangles, *57*
Solving Word Problems, *61*

Science
Acceleration and the Earth's Gravity, *66*
Tour the Circulatory System, *82*
Surviving a Lunar Crash, *97*

Social Studies
Balancing the Budget, *108*
Titanic: Unsinkable? *122*
War Letters, *128*

Favorite Web sites

Favorite Web sites

_____

_____

_____

_____

_____

_____

_____

_____

_____

_____

_____

_____

_____

_____

_____

_____

_____

Favorite Web sites

_____

_____

_____

_____

_____

_____

_____

_____

_____

_____

_____

_____

_____

_____

_____

_____

_____

Favorite Web sites

_____

_____

_____

_____

_____

_____

_____

_____

_____

_____

_____

_____

_____

_____

_____

_____

_____